QuickCook

QuickCook
Winter Warmers

Recipes by Jo McAuley

Every dish, three ways—you choose!
30 minutes | 20 minutes | 10 minutes

An Hachette UK Company
www.hachette.co.uk

First published in Great Britain in 2014 by Hamlyn,
a division of Octopus Publishing Group Ltd
Endeavour House, 189 Shaftesbury Avenue
London WC2H 8JY
www.octopusbooks.co.uk
www.octopusbooksusa.com

Distributed in the US by Hachette Book Group USA
237 Park Avenue, New York NY 10017 USA

Distributed in Canada by Canadian Manda Group
165 Dufferin Street, Toronto, Ontario, Canada M6K 3H6

ISBN 978-0-600-62707-4

Printed and bound in China.

10 9 8 7 6 5 4 3 2 1

Standard level kitchen cup and spoon measurements are used in all recipes.

Ovens should be preheated to the specified temperature. If using a convection oven,
follow the manufacturer's instructions for adjusting the time and temperature.
Broilers should also be preheated.

This book includes dishes made with nuts and nut derivatives. It is advisable for
those with known allergic reactions to nuts and nut derivatives and those who may
be potentially vulnerable to these allergies, such as pregnant and nursing mothers,
people with weakened immune systems, the elderly, babies, and children, to avoid
dishes made with nuts and nut oils.

It is also prudent to check the labels of prepared ingredients for the possible inclusion
of nut derivatives.

The U.S. Food and Drug Administration advises that eggs should not be consumed
raw. This book contains some dishes made with raw or lightly cooked eggs. It is
prudent for more vulnerable people, such as pregnant and nursing mothers, people
with weakened immune systems, the elderly, babies, and young children, to avoid
uncooked or lightly cooked dishes made with eggs.

Contents

Introduction

30 20 10—Quick, Quicker, Quickest

This book offers a new and flexible approach to planning meals for busy cooks, letting you choose the recipe option that best fits the time you have available. Inside, you will find 360 dishes that will inspire and motivate you to get cooking every day of the year. All the recipes take a maximum of 30 minutes to cook. Some take as little as 20 minutes and, amazingly, many take only 10 minutes. With a little preparation, you can easily try out one new recipe from this book each night and slowly you will be able to build a wide and exciting portfolio of recipes to suit your needs.

How Does it Work?

Every recipe in the QuickCook series can be cooked one of three ways: a 30-minute version, a 20-minute version, or a superquick-and-easy 10-minute version. At the beginning of each chapter, you'll find recipes listed by time. Choose a dish based on how much time you have and turn to that page.

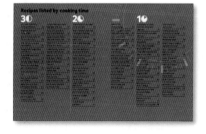

You'll find the main recipe in the middle of the page accompanied by a beautiful photograph, as well as two time-variation recipes below.

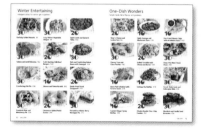

If you enjoy your chosen dish, why not go back and cook the other time-variation options at a later date? So, if you liked the 30-minute Roasted Chicken and Winter Vegetables but only have 10 minutes to spare this time around, you'll find a way to cook it using quick ingredients or clever shortcuts.

If you love the ingredients and flavors of the 10-minute Quick Pea and Leek Soup, why not try something more substantial, such as the 20-minute Potato, Pea, and Leek Soup, or be inspired to make a more elaborate version, the recpe for Winter Potato, Pea, and Leek Stew? Alternatively, browse through all 360 delicious recipes, find something that catches your eye, then cook the version that fits your time frame.

Or, for easy inspiration, turn to the gallery found on pages 12–19 to get an instant overview by themes, such as Winter Entertaining or One-Dish Wonders.

QuickCook Online

To make life easier, you can use the special code on each recipe page to e-mail yourself a recipe card for printing, or e-mail a text-only shopping list to your phone. Go to www.hamlynquickcook.com and enter the recipe code at the bottom of each page.

WIN-WINT-SYJ

Winter Warmers

When the winter months come rolling in, often all we want to do is curl up under warm blankets and not come out until the spring. Tempting although this option may seem, there are a lot of reasons to embrace the onset of winter and the touch of Jack Frost's icy fingers. For example, it's a time to make the most of all the fantastic seasonal produce, such as the first frost-sweetened parsnips and tall, scruffy-topped leeks.

It's Cold Outside ...

... so curl up by the fireside and enjoy some warming snacks and indulgent treats. Winter cooking is about getting the balance of warm spices, rich flavors, colors, and textures just right, whatever the occasion. Whether you are in need of a steaming bowl of rich Spiced Tomato and Chorizo Soup (page 108), a velvet-textured Comforting Fish Casserole (page 198) or even a light-up-the-senses slice of Fire and Ice Winter Berry Meringue Pie (page 272), you will find the recipe here. This is a book full of wet- and windy-day recipes created to tempt you out of hibernation, banish the winter blues, and invite you into the warm, culinary pleasures of your kitchen.

Build Up Your Winter Staples

As the cold winter approach, build up a stockpile of staple ingredients in the pantry or cupboards, refrigerator, and freezer. Not only will it save trekking to the stores in bad weather, but it will enable you to whip up delicious meals at short notice.

A supply of onions, garlic, potatoes, carrots, leeks, and celery is essential. If you have these, you have a great base for a quick soup or stew. And remember to keep a good array of bouillon cubes or, even better, homemade stock in the freezer, because these will add depth and flavor with minimum effort.

Canned food is also a great standby. Keep a selection of canned beans, such as chickpeas, lima beans, navy beans, kidney beans, and lentils. These will bulk out a meal and also add plenty of goodness. Canned fruits and vegetables are also great for quick-fix meals, and will count toward your five-a-day.

At a time of year when only the hardiest winter herbs can survive outside, a rack of dried herbs and spices is useful for adding flavor to everyday dishes, and they can be used to create deliciously exotic and inspiring meals.

Once you are well-stocked in the staples, you'll only need to buy occasional extras. For example, chopped pancetta for a hearty bowl of Italian Beans with Pancetta (page 106), a chunk of fresh ginger for an exotic Quick Carrot and Cilantro Stew (page 80), or some thinly sliced steak for an authentic-tasting Cowboy Beef and Bean Casserole (page 110).

Where possible, it is also worth cooking dishes in bulk and freezing the extra for future use. You'll be pleased you did when you can't get to the stores and want to feed people in a hurry. Take a look through the Hearty Soups and Stews chapter (pages 72–123) for more great inspiration.

Eat Yourself to Health This Winter

Providing meals packed with nutritious, energy-boosting ingredients means that you and yours will probably stay fit and healthy throughout the colder months, and in this book Winter Cold Busters (pages 124–175) is dedicated to achieving just that. It is, of course, important to eat a well-balanced diet at any time of year, but never more so than during the winter. This can be a time when your body and immune system are already weakened from lack of natural daylight and the effort of keeping warm and fighting off a variety of bugs and germs.

You can help to protect yourself from this onslaught with a combination of things. Try to get as much regular exercise as possible, make sure you are getting the right amount of sleep, drink plenty of water to stay hydrated, and eat a good and varied diet. This means consuming all the essential proteins, vitamins, fats, and minerals that may seem scarce in the winter, but that are vital in the quest to stay healthy.

The reduction in daylight hours can also take its toll and contribute to a deficiency in vitamin D, normally produced by the body when it is exposed to natural sunlight. Eating oily fish, such as mackerel, sardines, and herring, can help boost your vitamin D levels and, as a bonus, contain a high level of omega-3 fatty acids, which are essential for improving metabolism.

Iron deficiency can lead to fatigue and anemia, so it's a good idea to boost your intake by eating plenty of dark green vegetables, such as spinach and kale, red meats, oysters, mussels, lentils, and chickpeas, all of which have a naturally high iron content.

If you do succumb to a cold or flu, this chapter also has recipes to get you back on your feet faster than you can say "Jack Frost." Why not try a soothing bowl of Feed-a-Cold Chicken Soup (page 132), an endorphin-boosting Cold-Busting Chocolate Beef Chili (page 164), or a sinus-clearing Steamed Salmon with Chile and Ginger (page 138)?

It is a well-known fact that, combined with regular exercise, plenty of sleep, and staying hydrated, eating healthily can make a real difference to how your body and immune system cope, no matter how bad the winter weather gets. So help yourself stay in top form this and every winter, and hop over to the Winter Cold Busters chapter for some delicious healthy-eating inspiration.

Comforting Winter Warmers

As you'll see throughout this book, comfort food doesn't necessarily have to be carbohydrate-loaded, heavy meals, but it should have a feel-good effect and leave you satisfied. Different recipes will be comforting for different people, but, whatever your comfort food of choice, it has to suit the mood—whether that might be a desire for the simple pleasures of a deep bowlful of Pesto Spaghetti Meatballs (page 224) or the soothing comfort of Creamy Butternut and Sage Orzo (page 180). Or perhaps you want to bring back fond childhood memories of your grandmother's Beef Casserole with Parsnips (page 218), the culinary equivalent of crawling under a warm blanket. Whatever your prefer, you will find your perfect comfort-food recipe in the Comfort-Food Main Dishes chapter (pages 176–227).

Seasonal Winter Produce

It may have been said before, but it makes sense to eat foods that are in season. The wealth of fresh produce available in the supermarket all year round makes it easy to forget that certain fruits and vegetables are not actually homegrown during the winter. Check what should be available locally and ignor the rest. Take a look at the frozen, canned, and dried alternatives, and avoid buying the so-called "fresh" fruits and vegetables that have often traveled thousands of miles to reach your local supermarket. Instead, bring a ray of summer into your winter cooking by buying locally grown fruits and vegetables that have been frozen in season for use all year round. They will often contain more vitamins and minerals than their more-traveled counterparts, and they are also easier on your budget.

Although not exhaustive, here is a list of fresh produce in season during at least some of the winter months, and for which you will find recipes in this book.

Fruit: Apples, clementines, dates, figs, grapefruit, lemons, mandarins, oranges, pears, and rhubarb.

Vegetables: Beets, Brussels sprouts, cabbage, carrots, cauliflower, celeriac, celery, Jerusalem artichokes, leeks, lettuce, mushrooms, onions, parsnips, potatoes, radicchio, squash, sweet potatoes, watercress, and winter greens.

Fish and Seafood: Cod, crab, mackerel, mussels, oysters, and shrimp.

Put on an Apron ...

... and get baking! Cheer up those long winter days by raiding the Winter Desserts, Sweet Treats, and Drinks chapter (pages 228–279) and baking up a storm. What could be more wonderful than coming back from a brisk, frosty afternoon walk in the countryside and having a plate of warmed, freshly baked Cinnamon-Spiked Raisin Scones (page 256) or a mountain of Chunky Double Choc-Chip Cookies (page 252) on the table in less than 20 minutes? Why not have a change by swapping your ordinary cup of tea for an aromatic Irish Cream Cup of Chai (page 270), and giving the children Whipped Cream Hot Chocolate (page 270), minus the alcohol, of course? The delicious aroma of home-baked goodies is guaranteed to cheer everybody up, even on the grayest of days.

Classic Winter Warmers

Comfort foods to banish the winter blues.

Garlicky Broiled Mussels 36

Lazy Winter Vegetable Stew 98

Quick Lamb and Spinach Tikka 148

Salmon and Lentil Fish Cakes 162

Cold-Busting Mexican Hamburgers 164

Rich and Comforting Baked Beans with Sausages 184

Comforting Fish Casserole 198

Cheese and Onion on Toast 202

Quick-Fried Steak Stroganoff 210

Freeform Pear and Blackberry Pie 254

Cinnamon-Spiked Raisin Scones 256

Fire and Ice Winter Berry Meringue Pie 272

Children Will Love These

Culinary central heating for kids.

Skier's Cheese and
Bacon Tart 68

Quick Sausage and
Mushroom Stew 118

Pan-Fried Polenta Fries
with Arrabbiata Sauce 182

Cheesy Tuna and
Chive Pastries 190

Tortellini Casserole with
Cheese and Bacon 194

Deep-Pan Meat-Feast
Pizza 208

Quick Fish Schnitzel with
Tartar Sauce 214

Roast Beef Waffles 218

Greek-Style Lamb and
Eggplant Casserole 226

Toasted Ginger Syrup
Waffles 242

Chunky Double Choc-Chip
Cookies 252

Mandarin and Vanilla Seed
Brownies 258

Winter Entertaining

Indulgent dishes for winter get-togethers.

Onion and Mushroom Vol-au-Vents 40

Rock Oyster Kilpatrick with Shallots 42

Warm Fig and Prosciutto Salad with Gorgonzola 52

Beet Tarte Tatin with Goat Cheese 60

Spicy Sardine Linguine 174

Creamy Butternut and Sage Orzo 180

Beef Bourguignon 192

Cacciatore-Style Chicken and Salami Pasta 212

Quick Creamy Ham and Ricotta Cannelloni 216

Panettone and Butter Pudding with Raspberries 236

Brown Sugar Plum Turnovers 244

Melting Chocolate and Date Cakes 246

One-Dish Wonders

Simple meals full of flavor and goodness.

Quick Pea and Leek Soup 82

Peperonata-Style Pork and Chorizo Casserole 100

Italian Beans with Pancetta 106

Soupy Butternut Squash and Ham Rice Bowl 112

Bean, Bacon, and Cabbage Soup with Rosemary Pistou 114

Red Cabbage and Beet Stew 158

Spiced Cabbage and Bacon Pan-Fry 166

Cremini Mushroom and Spinach Pilaf 168

Quick Fish Stew with Chickpeas 170

Wintry Fruit Salad 234

Canned Cherry and Apricot Cobbler 268

Moist Chocolate Pear Cake 276

Hearty Meat Recipes

Satisfying feasts to warm up your menu.

Rosemary, Bacon, and Brie Muffins 46

Skier's Cheese and Bacon Tart 68

Lamb and Gnocchi Casserole 88

Spicy Black-Eyed Peas and Sausages 92

Spiced Tomato and Chorizo Soup 108

Cowboy Beef and Bean Casserole 110

Mexican Beef Chili Soup 122

Broiled Lamb with Kale and Spicy Tomato Salsa 136

Pork, Red Pepper, and Three-Bean Goulash 154

Crispy Pork Milanese with Root Vegetable Coleslaw 188

Spicy Sausage and Salsa Ciabattas 222

Pesto and Meatball Tagliatelle 224

Superhealthy Fish Feasts

Omega-rich delights to boost your metabolism.

Spiced Potted Crab with Whole-Wheat Toasts 28

Sweet Chili Roasted Salmon Rillettes with Blinis 32

Curried Moules Marinières 48

Warm Potato and Mackerel Salad 70

Coconut Fish Laksa with Lemon Grass 94

Jumbo Shrimp and Sweet Potato Curry 104

Smoked Salmon and Edamame Cups 128

Crispy Salmon Ramen 138

Poached Smoked Haddock with Fried Eggs 142

Mussel and Leek Carbonara 146

Tuna and Bulgur Wheat Bowl 152

Jumbo Shrimp Soba Noodles with Sweet-and-Sour Dressing 156

Cheering Chicken Dishes

Protein-packed meals to tempt you out of hibernation.

Smoked Duck with Clementine and Walnut Salad 64

Chicken and Spinach Stew 78

Jerk Chicken and Sweet Potato Soup 90

Chicken and Rice Soup in a Mug 96

Thai Chicken Noodle Broth 116

Feed-a-Cold Chicken Soup 132

Stir-Fried Lemon Chicken with Toasted Cashew Nuts 160

Chicken and Brie Puff Pie 186

Roasted Chicken and Winter Vegetables 196

Cajun-Spiced Turkey Meatballs 204

Creamy Chicken and Mushroom Rice 206

Feta-Stuffed Chicken with Chile and Capers 220

Eat Your Greens

Nourishing veggie meals crammed full of good stuff.

Beet and Horseradish Hummus 26

Chargrilled Eggplant and Garlic Bruschette 30

Fennel and Onion Soup with Melting Gruyère 38

Indian-Spiced Fritters with Mango Chutney 44

Leek and Chestnut Pancakes 62

Red Pepper Soup with Spicy Caraway and Chickpea Salsa 76

Quick Carrot and Cilantro Stew 80

Quick Parsnip and Lentil Dhal 86

Quick Mushroom and Garlic Tom Yum 102

Roasted Squash and Chickpea Stew 144

Quick Spiced Cauliflower Pilaf 150

Gnocchi Gratin with Sun-Dried Tomato and Mascarpone 200

QuickCook

Fireside Appetizers, Salads, and Bites

Recipes listed by cooking time

30

20

Homemade Jerusalem Artichoke Chips with Sage Salt

Serves 4

vegetable oil, for deep-frying
1 lb Jerusalem artichokes, scrubbed
2 teaspoons finely chopped sage
1 tablespoon salt, preferably flaky sea salt

- Heat the oil in a wide, deep skillet or saucepan to 350–375°F, or until a cube of bread thrown into the oil turns golden in about 1 minute.

- Slice the artichokes thinly, using a mandoline slicer, if possible.

- Carefully drop handfuls of the sliced artichokes into the oil and deep-fry for about 1 minute, or until the artichokes are golden. Remove with a slotted spoon and drain on paper towels. Repeat with the remaining artichokes.

- Combine the sage and salt. Transfer the chips into bowls and serve immediately, sprinkled with a pinch of the sage salt.

2 Warm Sage and Jerusalem Artichoke Salad

Heat 1 tablespoon olive oil with 2 tablespoons butter in a large skillet and add 1 lb scrubbed or peeled, thinly sliced Jerusalem artichokes. Cook over medium heat, turning occasionally, for 10–12 minutes, until softened and golden. Add 1 chopped garlic clove and 2 teaspoons chopped sage to the pan for the final 2 minutes, then season with salt and black pepper. Meanwhile, arrange a handful of mixed salad greens on each of 4 plates. Top with the golden artichoke and sage, then sprinkle with shaved Parmesan cheese and drizzle with a little extra virgin olive oil. Serve immediately, accompanied by wedges of lemon, if desired.

3 Jerusalem Artichoke and Sage Pithiviers

Cook 1 lb peeled and diced Jerusalem artichokes in a saucepan of lightly salted, boiling water for about 8 minutes, or until tender. Meanwhile, cook 2 trimmed and sliced leeks in a large skillet with 2 tablespoons butter, melted, over medium heat for 5–6 minutes, until softened. Unroll 2 sheets of ready-to-bake, chilled puff pastry and cut four 5 inch circles out of each one. Place 4 of the circles on a lightly greased baking sheet. Drain the artichokes, then return to the pan and mash lightly with the cooked leek, 3 oz Roquefort or other blue cheese, and 2 teaspoons chopped sage.

Spoon this mixture into the middle of the pastry circles. Brush the edges with a little beaten egg, top with the remaining 4 pastry circles, and press to seal. Brush with more beaten egg, make a small hole in the top of each one, and bake in a preheated oven, at 400°F, for 15–18 minutes, until puffed up and golden. Serve hot with mixed winter salad greens.

Beet and Horseradish Hummus

Serves 4–6

6 cooked beets, coarsely diced
2 tablespoons horseradish sauce
1 (15 oz) can chickpeas, rinsed
    and drained
½ teaspoon ground cumin
2 tablespoons olive oil
1 teaspoon lemon juice
salt and black pepper
chopped chives, to garnish

To serve
crème fraîche (optional)
pita breads, cut into strips

- Put the diced beets into the small bowl of a food processor with the horseradish, chickpeas, cumin, olive oil, lemon juice, and a generous pinch of salt and black pepper. Blend until almost smooth.

- Spoon into bowls and top with a dollop of crème fraîche, if desired. Garnish with the chopped herbs and serve with strips of pita bread.

20 Warm Beet Salad with Horseradish

Dressing Heat 1 tablespoon oil in a skillet and cook 2 sliced garlic cloves over low heat for 2 minutes, until just softened. Stir in 1 teaspoon cumin seeds and heat for another minute, then add 10 cooked beets, cut into wedges. Warm for 3–4 minutes, then remove from the heat and toss briefly with 4 cups arugula leaves. Meanwhile, combine 2 teaspoons horseradish sauce with 1 teaspoon lemon juice, 3 tablespoons crème fraîche, and 2 teaspoons chopped chives and season to taste. Pile the warm salad into dishes and drizzle with the dressing to serve.

30 Beet Soup with Horseradish

Heat 2 tablespoons olive oil in a large saucepan and cook 2 chopped shallots, 2 chopped garlic cloves, and ½ teaspoon cumin seeds over medium heat, for 4–5 minutes, stirring occasionally, until softened. Add 15 peeled and diced beets (about 1½ lb). Pour 3 cups hot chicken or vegetable stock into the pan and simmer for about 20 minutes, until the beets are tender. Meanwhile, combine 2 teaspoons horseradish sauce with 2 tablespoons crème fraîche and 1 teaspoon lemon juice, then season to taste. Blend the soup until smooth, then ladle into bowls and serve with a dollop of horseradish cream and chopped chives or parsley to garnish.

30 Spiced Potted Crab with Whole-Wheat Toasts

Serves 4

1½ sticks butter, melted
  and cooled
½ teaspoon sweet paprika
pinch of ground cayenne pepper
½ teaspoon ground mace
2 teaspoons lemon juice
2 tablespoons finely chopped
  parsley (optional)
14 oz crabmeat
salt and black pepper

To serve

whole-wheat toast
lemon wedges (optional)

- Put the melted butter into a bowl with the spices, lemon juice, parsley, if using, and a pinch of salt and black pepper. Beat the ingredients together.

- Add the crabmeat to the spiced butter and beat again. Spoon into 4 ramekins, then cover with plastic wrap and chill for at least 20 minutes, or until required.

- When ready, prepare the toast and serve with the potted crab and lemon wedges, if desired.

---

10 Lemony Spiced Crab Mayonnaise

In a bowl, gently combine 14 oz crabmeat with ¼ cup mayonnaise, 1 teaspoon sweet paprika, a pinch of cayenne pepper, ½ teaspoon ground mace, 2 teaspoons lemon juice, and 1 tablespoon chopped parsley. Season with black pepper, mix well, and serve immediately with whole-wheat toast. Alternatively, chill until required.

20 Spiced Crab Cocktail with

Crostini Pile 2 sliced small butterhead lettuce into 4 attractive serving bowls with a handful of watercress. Arrange 1 peeled, pitted, and sliced avocado over the top with 8 quartered cherry tomatoes. Flake 12 oz of crabmeat over the salads. For the dressing, combine ¼ cup mayonnaise with 2 teaspoons ketchup,

2 teaspoons lemon juice, and the spices and seasoning from the main recipe. Cut 1 small French bread into thin slices and toast until crisp and golden. Serve the crab cocktail with the crostini and the mayonnaise dressing.

Chargrilled Eggplant and Garlic Bruschette

Serves 4

2 eggplants
2 tablespoons olive oil
4 thick slices of country-style
  bread
1 garlic clove, cut in half
⅔ cup herbed cream cheese,
  such as Boursin
4 small handfuls of watercress
  leaves or baby spinach
salt and black pepper
chili or extra olive oil, to drizzle
  (optional)

- Cut the eggplants into slices about ¼ inch thick and brush with the olive oil.

- Place a ridged grill pan over medium heat and, when hot, chargrill the eggplant slices in 3 batches for 5–6 minutes, turning once, until softened and nicely charred.

- Meanwhile, toast the bread until golden. Lightly rub one side of the toast with the cut side of the garlic, then season lightly with salt and black pepper. Spread thickly with the cream cheese.

- Arrange the eggplant over the cheese and top each slice with a small handful of watercress leaves or spinach.

- Serve drizzled with a little chili or olive oil, if desired.

Chargrilled Vegetable and Spinach Salad

Toast 2 tablespoons pine nuts in a dry skillet for 3–4 minutes, shaking frequently, until golden. Transfer to a plate and set aside to cool. Toast 4 slices of country-style bread and spread thickly with ⅔ cup herbed cream cheese, such as Boursin. Arrange a handful of baby spinach on each of 4 serving plates. Combine 8 oz of store-bought mixed chargrilled antipasti, such as eggplant, mushrooms, roasted peppers, and artichokes, and sprinkle with the leaves. Sprinkle with the toasted pine nuts and serve immediately with the cheesy toasts.

Chargrilled Eggplant with Cornmeal

Put 4 chorizo cooking sausages into a small baking pan and roast in a preheated oven, at 400°F, for 10–15 minutes, or according to the package directions, until cooked and golden. Chargrill the eggplants following the main recipe, and keep warm. Melt 1 stick butter in a small saucepan over low heat and add 2 chopped garlic cloves, ½ teaspoon dried red pepper flakes (optional), and 1 teaspoon chopped sage leaves. Heat gently for 3–4 minutes, until the garlic is softened but not browned. Set aside and keep warm. Bring 2¼ cups vegetable stock to a boil and add ⅔ cup instant cornmeal or polenta in a steady stream, whisking constantly to prevent lumps from forming. Cook over low heat for about 5 minutes, or according to package directions, until thickened. Remove from the heat and add ⅓ cup herbed cream cheese, such as Boursin, and beat until smooth. Season to taste. Spoon the cornmeal into dishes, arrange the eggplants and chorizo sausages alongside, and drizzle with the garlicky butter to serve.

Sweet Chili Roasted Salmon Rillettes with Blinis

Serves 4–6

30–36 cocktail-size blinis

8 oz prepared roasted
salmon fillets

½ cup cream cheese

1–2 teaspoons sweet chili sauce,
according to taste

2–3 teaspoons lemon juice,
according to taste

salt and black pepper

snipped chives or cilantro,
to garnish (optional)

- Wrap the blinis in aluminum foil and warm them in a preheated oven, at 350°F, or according to the package directions.

- Meanwhile, remove the skin from the salmon and flake the flesh into a bowl. Add the remaining ingredients and mash with a fork to the desired consistency. (This can be done in a food processor, if you prefer.) Season to taste.

- Serve the pâté with the warm blinis, garnishing with the chives, if desired.

2 Giant Smoked Salmon and Sweet Chili Blinis

Prepare the blini batter following the directions for the 30-minute recipe. Melt 1 tablespoon of butter in a large, nonstick saucepan. Using half the batter, pour 3 dollops into the pan to make 3 large blinis. Cook for 2–3 minutes, until lightly golden, then flip over and cook for another minute. Set aside and keep warm while you make another 3 blinis. Put ½ cup cream cheese into a small bowl with 1 tablespoon sweet chili sauce, 1 teaspoon lemon juice, 2 teaspoons chopped cilantro, and a pinch of salt and black pepper. Beat together, then spread thickly over the blinis. Top with thin layers of smoked salmon to serve.

3 Sweet Chili Canapé Blinis with Rillettes

Sift 1 cup all-purpose flour, 1 teaspoon baking powder, and a pinch of salt into a bowl, then make a well in the middle. Separate 1 extra-large egg and add the yolk to the flour with ¾ cup milk, 1 tablespoon chopped chives or cilantro, 1 tablespoon sweet chili sauce, a pinch of black pepper, and 2 tablespoons crème fraîche. Whisk the mixture, gradually incorporating the flour from the sides, until a smooth batter forms. Whisk the egg white in a clean bowl until stiff peaks form, then fold into the batter. Put 1 tablespoon butter into a large, nonstick skillet or pancake pan over medium heat. When melted, drop small spoonfuls of the batter into the pan and cook for about 2 minutes, or until bubbles begin to form on the surface of the blinis and the underside is lightly golden. Flip over and cook the other side for 30–60 seconds, until lightly golden. Set aside and keep warm while you make about another 30 blinis in the same way, adding extra butter each time, if necessary. Meanwhile, prepare the salmon rillettes following the main recipe. Serve the canapé blinis with the prepared rillettes.

Warm Mushroom Salad Crostini

Serves 4

6 tablespoons butter

2 garlic cloves, chopped

1 tablespoon chopped herbs, such as chervil, parsley, tarragon, and chives

8 oz mixed mushrooms, such as portobello, porcini, or chanterelle, thickly sliced

sourdough or country-style bread, thinly sliced

- Melt the butter in a large skillet with the garlic and herbs until just beginning to foam. Add the mushrooms and sauté over medium heat for 4–5 minutes, until soft and golden.

- Meanwhile, heat a ridged grill pan. When hot, toast the bread in it until golden and nicely charred. To serve, arrange the crostini on plates and spoon the mushrooms over the top.

20 Creamy Baked Eggs and Mushrooms

Sauté the mushrooms following the main recipe. Meanwhile, mix ⅔ cup heavy cream in a bowl with a pinch of salt and black pepper. Stir the mushrooms into the cream, then divide among 4 ovenproof ramekins. Crack an egg into each ramekin and place the dishes in a roasting pan. Fill the pan halfway with hot water, then place in a preheated oven, at 400°F, for 7–8 minutes, until the eggs are set but the yolk is still slightly runny. Remove from the oven and serve immediately with slices of toasted sourdough.

30 Roasted Portobello Mushrooms in Red Wine

Put 12 small portobello mushrooms into a bowl and toss with 3 tablespoons olive oil, ½ cup full-bodied red wine, 2 chopped garlic cloves, 2 tablespoons chopped parsley, and a generous pinch of salt and black pepper. Arrange stem side up in a snug-fitting, ovenproof dish and roast in a preheated oven, at 375°F, for about 15 minutes, until softened. Serve spooned over toasted sourdough with the warm juices and plenty of extra chopped parsley.

3⬤ Garlicky Broiled Mussels

Serves 4

4 tablespoons butter
2 shallots, chopped
3 garlic cloves, chopped
½ cup dry white wine
1¼ lb mussels, debearded and scrubbed
½ cup dried bread crumbs
2 tablespoons finely chopped parsley
1 teaspoon finely grated lemon zest
2 tablespoons freshly grated Parmesan cheese
1 tablespoon olive oil

- Melt the butter in a large saucepan over medium-low heat and cook the shallots and 2 of the garlic cloves for 5–6 minutes, until softened. Pour in the wine, increase the heat slightly, and bring to a boil.

- Transfer the mussels to the pan, discarding any that won't close when sharply tapped, then cover and simmer gently for 3–5 minutes, shaking the pan occasionally, until the shells are opened. Discard any that remain closed. Set aside until cool enough to handle.

- Meanwhile, put the bread crumbs in a bowl with the parsley, remaining garlic, lemon zest, Parmesan, and oil and mix well.

- Discard the empty half shell from each mussel and arrange the mussels in a single layer on a large baking sheet.

- Spoon the bread crumb mixture neatly over the mussels and cook under a preheated medium broiler for 2–3 minutes, or until the bread crumbs are crisp and golden.

1⬤ Mussels in Garlic Butter Sauce

Melt 4 tablespoons butter in a skillet with 2 chopped shallots and 3 chopped garlic cloves. Cook over low heat for 2–3 minutes, then add ⅓ cup dry white wine and 2 teaspoons Pernod (optional). Simmer for 3–4 minutes. Transfer 12 oz cooked, shelled mussels to the pan and reheat quickly. Remove from the heat and stir in 2 tablespoons heavy cream. Season, sprinkle with 2 tablespoons chopped parsley, spoon into dishes, and serve.

2⬤ Herbed Garlic Butter Mussel

Packages Melt 4 tablespoons butter in a skillet with 2 chopped garlic cloves for 2–3 minutes, until softened. Add 2 tablespoons chopped parsley, 1 teaspoon Pernod (optional), and 8 oz cooked, shelled mussels. Stir for 1 minute, then remove from the heat. Brush 4 large sheets of phyllo pastry with melted butter, then fold in half. Spoon the mussels onto one end of each pastry strip, then fold up to form brick-shape packages, tucking in the edges as you fold. Melt 2 tablespoons butter in a clean skillet with 1 tablespoon olive oil and cook the packages for 8–10 minutes, turning occasionally, until crisp and golden. Serve with salad greens and French bread.

30 Fennel and Onion Soup with Melting Gruyère

Serves 4

6 tablespoons butter
1 bulb of fennel, thinly sliced
2 large onions, halved and
  thinly sliced
2 garlic cloves, coarsely chopped
2 teaspoons chopped thyme
1 teaspoon dark brown sugar
3 tablespoons brandy or dry sherry
3 cups hot beef stock
1 teaspoon dark soy sauce
  (optional)
4 small slices of sourdough bread
1 cup grated Gruyère cheese or
  Swiss cheese
salt and black pepper

- Melt the butter in a large saucepan over medium-low heat and cook the fennel, onions, garlic, thyme, and sugar for about 20 minutes, stirring occasionally, until soft and slightly caramelized.

- Pour in the brandy or sherry and heat until completely evaporated. Add the stock and soy sauce, if using, and bring to a boil, then simmer gently for about 5 minutes. Season to taste.

- Meanwhile, top the slices of sourdough with the grated cheese and arrange on an aluminum foil-lined broiler rack. Place under a preheated medium-hot broiler for 2–3 minutes, until the cheese is melting.

- To serve, ladle the soup into bowls and top with the Gruyère toasts.

10 Quick Fennel and Gruyère Salad

Slice 1 trimmed bulb of fennel thinly, using a mandoline slicer, if possible. Place in a bowl with 1 thinly sliced celery stick, 1 thinly sliced red onion, 1 peeled, cored, and thinly sliced sweet, crisp apple and 4 cups mixed salad greens. Drizzle with 2 tablespoons olive oil and 2 teaspoons lemon juice. Season with salt and black pepper, then toss lightly to coat. Pile onto serving plates and top with 2 oz Gruyère cheese, shaved, and 1 teaspoon coarsely chopped fennel fronds or dill. Serve the salad immediately.

20 Pan-Fried Fennel and Onion Salad with Gruyère Toasts

Cut 1 bulb of trimmed fennel into thin wedges. Melt 4 tablespoons butter in a large skillet and sauté the fennel and 1 sliced red onion over medium heat for about 10 minutes, turning occasionally, until slightly softened and golden. Stir in 1 teaspoon fennel seeds, 1 teaspoon chopped thyme, and a sprinkling of salt and black pepper. Pour in 2 tablespoons Pernod or pastis and simmer until completely evaporated. Remove from the heat and toss briefly with 2 handfuls frisée-style salad greens. Pile onto plates and serve topped with the Gruyère toasts from the main recipe.

20 Onion and Mushroom Vol-au-Vents

Makes 16

16 frozen vol-au-vent shells
  or puff pastry stamped into
  16 circles
4 tablespoons butter
1 small onion, finely chopped
1 garlic clove, chopped
8 oz mixed mushrooms,
  thinly sliced
½ cup mascarpone cheese
2 teaspoons chopped herbs, such
  as tarragon, chervil, and chives,
  plus extra to garnish (optional)
salt and black pepper

• Line a baking sheet with parchment paper. Arrange the vol-au-vent shells on it and bake in a preheated oven, at 425°F, for 10–12 minutes, or according to the package directions, until crisp and golden.

• Meanwhile, melt the butter in a skillet and cook the onion and garlic over medium heat for 6–7 minutes, stirring occasionally, until softened and golden. Add the mushrooms and sauté for another 3–4 minutes, until softened.

• Stir the mascarpone and herbs into the skillet, add a pinch of salt and black pepper, then remove from the heat.

• Spoon the filling into the pastry shells and serve warm, garnished with freshly snipped chives, if desired.

10 Onion and Mushroom Focaccia

Sprinkle 2 cups thinly sliced cremini mushrooms on top of a loaf of focaccia or similar flat bread. Top with half a thinly sliced red onion, drizzle with 1 tablespoon olive oil, and sprinkle with ½ teaspoon dried thyme. Place in a preheated oven, at 400°F, for 6–7 minutes, until hot and lightly browned. Cut into strips to serve.

30 Onion and Mushroom Tart

Score a ¾ inch border around the edge of a chilled sheet of ready-to-bake puff pastry and put onto a baking sheet lined with parchment paper. Mix 1 tablespoon chopped chives, 2 tablespoons caramelized onions, and a pinch of salt and black pepper into 3 tablespoons mascarpone. Spread evenly over the pastry, keeping within the border. Sprinkle 2 cups thinly sliced mushrooms and half a thinly sliced red onion over the top, and sprinkle with 2 tablespoons freshly grated Parmesan cheese. Bake in a preheated oven, at 400°F, for about 15–20 minutes, until crisp and golden. Serve with plenty of green salad.

30 Rock Oyster Kilpatrick with Shallots

Serves 4

coarse sea salt

16 large rock oysters

1 tablespoon olive oil

4 zestless bacon slices, finely chopped

2 banana shallots, finely chopped

2 tablespoons flat leaf parsley, chopped

2 teaspoons Worcestershire sauce

few drops of Tabasco sauce (optional)

1 cup fresh bread crumbs

lemon wedges, to serve (optional)

- Cover a baking sheet with a thick layer of coarse sea salt.

- Wrap one hand in a dish towel and hold an oyster in it, flat side up, with the "hinge" pointing toward you. Insert the tip of an oyster knife into the hinge, force it into the gap, then twist the knife until the shell opens. Push the knife in deeper and run it along the top of the shell to cut through the muscle that attaches the oyster to it. Discard the top shell. Remove any grit from the oyster, being careful to avoid losing any of the liquid inside the shell. Run the knife underneath the oyster to cut through the muscle attached to the bottom shell. Place the open oyster on the baking sheet and repeat this process with the remaining oysters.

- Heat the oil in a skillet and cook the bacon for 6–7 minutes, stirring occasionally. Drain on paper towels. Sauté the shallots in the bacon fat over medium-low heat for 4–5 minutes. Transfer to a bowl and add the bacon, parsley, and Worcestershire sauce, and Tabasco, if desired. Mix well.

- Return the pan to the heat and add the bread crumbs with a little more oil, if needed. Sauté for 4–5 minutes. Add to the bacon mixture and stir well. Spoon the topping over the oysters and cook under a preheated medium-hot broiler for 1–2 minutes. Serve immediately with lemon wedges, if desired.

1 Rock Oysters with Shallot Vinegar

Chop 2 shallots and mix with 3 tablespoons red wine vinegar and a pinch of salt and sugar. Open 12–16 oysters, as above, and arrange on 4 serving plates, using a bed of rock salt to keep them upright if you prefer. Serve with a small dish of shallot vinegar and Tabasco sauce.

2 Simple Broiled Oysters with Shallots

Open 12–16 oysters, as in the main recipe. Arrange them on a baking sheet covered with rock salt. Sprinkle 2 finely chopped slices of prosciutto over the oysters, followed by 2 finely chopped shallots. Top each one with a drop of Worcestershire sauce and cook under a preheated medium-hot broiler for 1–2 minutes. Transfer to serving plates and serve immediately with a few drops of Tabasco sauce, if desired.

 # Indian-Spiced Fritters with Mango Chutney

Serves 4

2 eggs

3 sweet potatoes, peeled and coarsely grated

1 onion, thinly sliced

2 teaspoons peeled and freshly grated ginger root

1¼ cups all-purpose flour

1 teaspoon cumin seeds

1 teaspoon ground coriander

½ teaspoon ground turmeric (optional)

¼ teaspoon cayenne pepper

3 tablespoons vegetable oil

salt and black pepper

cilantro leaves, to garnish

mango chutney, to serve

- Beat the eggs in a bowl. Add the sweet potatoes, onion, and ginger and mix well. Sprinkle with the flour, spices, and seasoning and mix really well.

- Heat the oil in a large skillet and place large spoonfuls of the mixture in the pan, flattening slightly with the back of a spatula. Cook for 5–6 minutes over medium heat, turning once, until crisp and golden. Drain on paper towels and keep warm. Repeat with remaining mixture.

- Arrange the fritters on plates, garnish with cilantro leaves, and serve with mango chutney.

---

1 Poppadums with Indian Spices and Mango Chutney Heat 1½ inches of vegetable oil in a deep skillet to 350–375°F, or until a cube of bread browns in 1 minute. Deep-fry 8 poppadums, one at a time, for 30–45 seconds, or according to the package directions, until puffed and crisp. Drain on paper towels. Combine ½ teaspoon each of ground cumin and coriander with a pinch of hot chili powder and ¼ teaspoon ground turmeric. Dust the poppadums in the spice mix and serve with mango chutney and Indian pickles.

3 Indian-Spiced Scones with Mango Chutney Put 1⅔ cups all-purpose flour in a bowl, add 2½ teaspoons baking powder, 1 teaspoon salt, 1 teaspoon each of ground cumin and coriander, ½ teaspoon ground turmeric, and ¼ teaspoon hot chili powder. Mix well. Add 6 tablespoons butter, diced, and rub in with the fingertips until the mixture resembles fine bread crumbs. Add half a finely chopped red onion, 2 tablespoons chopped cilantro, 2 tablespoons mango chutney, 1 extra-large beaten egg, and 3–4 tablespoons of milk—just enough to form a soft dough. Turn the dough onto a lightly floured work surface and roll out to a thickness of ¾ inch. Using a 2½ inch cutter, stamp out 8 circles. Place on a baking sheet lined with parchment paper and bake in a preheated oven, at 425°F, for about 15 minutes, until risen and golden. Transfer to a wire rack to cool slightly, then serve warm with a tray of mango chutney and Indian-style pickles.

Rosemary, Bacon, and Brie Muffins

Serves 8

3 oz zestless bacon slices, finely chopped

1¾ cups all-purpose flour

1½ teaspoons baking powder

1 teaspoon baking soda

1 teaspoon sweet paprika

2 extra-large eggs

¼ teaspoon black pepper

pinch of salt

2 teaspoons finely chopped rosemary

⅔ cup milk

6 tablespoons butter, melted

4 oz firm Brie cheese, cut into cubes

- Cook the bacon in a large skillet over high heat for 3–4 minutes, stirring occasionally, until golden. Drain on paper towels.

- Meanwhile, sift the flour into a large bowl with the baking powder, baking soda, and paprika.

- Break the eggs into a small bowl and beat lightly. Add the black pepper, salt, rosemary, milk, and melted butter and whisk together. Pour the mixture into the dry ingredients, add two-thirds of both the Brie and cooked bacon, and stir until barely combined.

- Butter a 12-section muffin pan. Divide the batter among the prepared cups, top with the remaining bacon and Brie, and bake in a preheated oven, at 400°F, for 18–22 minutes, until risen and golden. Serve warm.

1 ○ Rosemary and Brie Flatbreads

Melt 4 tablespoons butter in a small saucepan with 1 crushed garlic clove, 2 teaspoons chopped rosemary, 1 teaspoon sweet paprika, and a generous pinch of black pepper. Warm gently until the butter begins to froth, then set aside. Meanwhile, toast 6 pita breads, flatbreads, or thick wraps until lightly golden, and slice 7 oz Brie. Brush the top of each bread with the flavored butter, add a few slices of Brie, and serve immediately.

2 ○ Rosemary and Brie Ciabatta

Make 3–4 incisions in the top of 6 ciabatta rolls, being careful not to cut all the way through. Put 1 stick butter, softened, into a bowl with 1 clove crushed garlic, 1 teaspoon sweet paprika, 2 teaspoons chopped rosemary, and plenty of ground black pepper. Mash well with a fork. Spread the rosemary butter inside the ciabatta incisions, then push a small slice of firm Brie into each one. Wrap each roll loosely in aluminum foil and bake in a preheated oven, at 350°F, for about 12 minutes, opening the foil for the final 2 minutes. The rolls should be lightly golden and the cheese melted. Serve hot.

 Curried Moules Marinières

Serves 4

2 tablespoons vegetable oil
1 onion, halved and finely sliced
1 inch piece of fresh ginger root,
  peeled and chopped
1 garlic clove, finely sliced
1 tablespoon medium curry paste
1 cup lager or dry white wine
3 tablespoons coconut milk
2 lb mussels, debearded
  and scrubbed
salt and black pepper
coarsely chopped cilantro,
  to garnish

- Heat the oil in a large saucepan and cook the onion for 4–5 minutes, until beginning to soften. Add the ginger and garlic and cook for 2–3 minutes, until softened.

- Stir in the curry paste and heat for 1 minute. Pour in the lager or wine and coconut milk, season, and stir to combine. Simmer for 3–4 minutes, then add the mussels and stir again.

- Cover the pan with a tight-fitting lid and simmer gently for 3–4 minutes, shaking the pan occasionally, until the mussels are open.

- Discard any mussels that have not opened, then spoon the remainder and their broth into warm dishes. Garnish with the chopped cilantro and serve immediately with a large bowl for the empty shells.

10 Curried Mussel Chapattis

Heat 2 tablespoons vegetable oil in a large skillet and add 2 halved and sliced shallots, 1 crushed garlic clove, and 1 teaspoon finely grated ginger root. Cook for 3–4 minutes over medium-low heat, until softened and lightly golden. Meanwhile, warm 4 chapattis according to the package directions. Stir 2 tablespoons mild curry paste into the shallots and stir over the heat for 1 minute. Pour 1¼ cups coconut milk into the pan and bring to a boil. Transfer 1 lb cooked, shelled mussels into the pan and stir as they heat through. Remove the pan from the heat and sprinkle with 2 tablespoons chopped cilantro. To serve, place the chapattis on plates and spoon the curried mussels on top.

30 Mini Mussel and Coconut Curry

Pies Make the curried mussels following the 10-minute recipe, increasing the coconut milk to 1¾ cups, then stir in the cilantro. Meanwhile, roll out 1 sheet of store-bought puff pastry to about ¼ inch. Cut into 4 circles ½ inch larger than 4 ovenproof ramekins. Spoon the mussels and sauce into the ramekins and top each with a pastry circle, letting it overhang slightly. Brush with beaten egg, cut a slit in the top of the pastry, and sprinkle with black mustard or onion seeds. Bake in a preheated oven, at 400°F, for 15–18 minutes.

30 Golden Fried Mozzarella Balls with Chili Jam

Serves 4

20 chilled mini mozzarella
  balls, drained
2 tablespoons flour
1 extra-large egg, lightly beaten
¾ cup dried bread crumbs
oil, for deep-frying
sweet chili jam, to serve

- Pat the mozzarella balls dry on paper towels.

- Put the flour, egg, and bread crumbs into 3 shallow dishes.

- Roll the mozzarella balls first in the flour, then in the egg, and finally in the bread crumbs, making sure they are well coated. Arrange in a single layer on a baking sheet and put into the freezer for 15 minutes.

- Meanwhile, heat 1½ inches of oil in a deep skillet or saucepan to 350–375°F, or until a cube of bread browns in 1 minute.

- Remove the baking sheet from the freezer and use a slotted spoon to carefully lower the mozzarella balls into the hot oil, a few at a time. Cook for about 60 seconds, or until they are crisp and golden. Drain on paper towels and keep warm. Repeat with the remaining balls and serve hot with sweet chili jam for dipping.

---

10 Chili Cheese Dip and Dippers

Put 2 teaspoons sweet paprika into a small bowl with 1 teaspoon dried oregano, ½ teaspoon dried garlic granules, and a generous pinch of cayenne pepper, salt, and black pepper. Brush 3 soft flour tortillas with a little vegetable oil and sprinkle with the prepared spice blend to coat lightly. Cut into triangles and arrange in a single layer on a large baking sheet. Bake in a preheated oven, at 400°F, for 6–7 minutes, until crisp and lightly golden. Meanwhile, combine ⅔ cup cream cheese in a bowl with 2 tablespoons sweet chili jam and 2 teaspoons chopped chives. Transfer the baked dippers to a wire rack until crisp, then serve with the chili cheese dip.

20 Baked Chili Cheese Fondue

Remove any plastic packaging from a whole Camembert or Brie cheese in a wooden box. Return it to the wooden box and cut several small slits in the surface of the cheese. Push 1 sliced garlic clove into the slits with a few small thyme sprigs and 1 seeded and sliced mild red chile. Bake in a preheated oven, at 400°F, for 12–15 minutes, until the cheese is melting. Serve with plenty of crusty bread and a bowl of chili jam, if desired.

Warm Fig and Prosciutto Salad with Gorgonzola

Serves 4

2 tablespoons olive oil
2 banana shallots, finely chopped
2 garlic cloves, finely chopped
2 teaspoons raspberry vinegar
8 small, ripe but firm figs
⅔ cup crumbled Gorgonzola
  cheese or other blue cheese
4 cups arugula leaves
8 slices prosciutto or other
  wafer-thin ham
salt and black pepper
lightly crushed toasted hazelnuts,
  to garnish (optional)

- Put the oil in a small skillet over medium-low heat. When hot, add the shallots and garlic and sauté for 4–5 minutes, until softened. Remove from the heat and whisk in the raspberry vinegar plus a pinch of salt and black pepper.

- Meanwhile, use a sharp knife to score a cross into the top of the figs. Pry them open and fill with the Gorgonzola. Place on a baking sheet, drizzle with a little oil, and put under a preheated medium-hot broiler for 4–5 minutes, until melting and lightly browned.

- Arrange the arugula leaves on 4 plates and top with the warm figs and slices of ham. Drizzle with the warm dressing and serve immediately, sprinkled with toasted hazelnuts, if desired, and a pinch of black pepper.

---

10 Melting Gorgonzola, Fig and Prosciutto Packages Cut 2 ripe, firm figs into 4 slices. Put 4 slices of prosciutto onto a clean work surface and place another 4 slices on top at right angles to form crosses. Slice 4 oz Gorgonzola or other blue cheese and place in the center of each cross, followed by 2 slices of fig for each cross. Sprinkle with a few lightly crushed, toasted hazelnuts, then fold the ham over the filling to form 4 packages. Heat 1 tablespoon oil in a large, nonstick skillet and cook for 3–4 minutes, turning once, until crisp and golden. Serve the packages with a dressed arugula salad.

30 Crispy Gorgonzola and Cured Ham Flatbreads Put 2 baking sheets into a preheated oven, at 425°F. Put 1⅔ cups all-purpose flour into a bowl with ¾ teaspoon active dry yeast and ½ teaspoon salt. Pour in ½ cup lukewarm water and 2 teaspoons olive oil. Mix to form a soft dough, then transfer to a floured work surface and knead for 5–8 minutes, until smooth. Divide into 4 equal pieces, then roll them into balls. Using a rolling pin, roll each ball into a really thin oval shape about 11 x 6 inches. Place the flatbreads on the hot baking sheets, drizzle a teaspoon of olive oil over each one, and sprinkle with a pinch of sea salt. Bake for 5–7 minutes, until the flatbreads are crisp. Top each one with 2 thin slices of Gorgonzola and 2 wafer-thin slices of cured ham, such as prosciutto, and serve immediately, sprinkled with a small handful of arugula leaves, if desired.

WIN-FIRE-PUO

30 Spiced Pear and Stilton Tarts with Watercress

Serves 4

2 tablespoons butter, melted,
plus extra for greasing
1 sheet ready-to-bake puff
pastry, chilled
flour, for dusting
2 ripe but firm pears
¼ teaspoon ground cloves
pinch of ground allspice
¼ teaspoon ground black pepper
½ cup Stilton or other
blue cheese
¼ cup walnut pieces
1 teaspoon thyme leaves
1 red chile, seeded and chopped
(optional)

To serve

watercress
maple syrup (optional)

- Lightly grease a baking sheet. Roll out the pastry on a lightly floured work surface to the thickness of about ¼ inch. Using a 5 inch saucer as a template, cut out 4 circles and place them on the prepared baking sheet.

- Brush the circles with the melted butter and, using the tip of a sharp knife and a slightly smaller saucer, score a ½ inch border around the edge of each one. Bake in a preheated oven, at 400°F, for about 8 minutes, until pale golden.

- Meanwhile, peel, core, and slice the pears. Combine the cloves, allspice, and black pepper in a bowl.

- Remove the pastries from the oven and arrange the pear slices on them, keeping within the border. Dust lightly with the spices, then sprinkle with the Stilton, walnuts, and thyme leaves. Dot with the chile, if using.

- Return the pastries to the oven for another 8–10 minutes, until crisp and golden. Serve with a handful of watercress leaves and drizzled with a little maple syrup, if desired.

 Stilton, Pear, and Watercress Salad
Peel, core, and slice 2 ripe, firm pears. Put a handful of watercress onto 4 plates and top with the pears. Sprinkle with ⅔ cup crumbled Stilton or other blue cheese, ¼ cup walnut pieces, 1 seeded and finely chopped red chile, and 1 teaspoon thyme leaves. Whisk 3 tablespoons walnut oil with 2 teaspoons red wine vinegar and 1 teaspoon maple syrup. Serve the salad drizzled with the dressing.

 Warm Pears with Stilton and Watercress Peel, quarter, and core 3 ripe but firm pears. Melt 4 tablespoons butter in a nonstick skillet with 1 tablespoon maple syrup and 1 seeded and finely chopped red chile (optional) over medium-low heat. Add the pear quarters and sauté gently for 3–5 minutes, until tender and lightly caramelized. Sprinkle with the spices from the main recipe and toss gently for another minute. Set aside to cool slightly.

Put a handful of watercress onto 4 plates and arrange the warm pears on top. Drizzle with the warm dressing, sprinkle with ½ cup crumbled Stilton or other blue cheese and ¼ cup lightly crushed walnuts, and serve immediately.

20 Winter Herb Pesto and Goat Cheese Ravioli

Serves 4

2 tablespoons blanched hazelnuts
¼ cup chopped herbs, such as
   parsley, thyme, rosemary, sage
1 cup arugula leaves
1 small garlic clove, chopped
½ cup extra virgin olive oil
1 teaspoon lemon juice
2 tablespoons freshly grated hard
   goat cheese or Parmesan
   cheese, plus extra to serve
10 oz fresh ravioli or tortellini,
   such as butternut squash
   and herb
salt and black pepper

- Put a dry skillet over medium heat and toast the hazelnuts for 4–5 minutes, shaking the pan frequently, until lightly golden. Transfer to a plate and set aside to cool.

- Put the herbs, arugula, garlic, and cooled hazelnuts into a small food processor and pulse briefly until coarsely chopped. With the motor running, add the olive oil in a steady stream and blend until almost smooth.

- Scrape the pesto into a bowl, then stir in the lemon juice and grated cheese and season to taste.

- Cook the ravioli in a large saucepan of salted boiling water for 2–3 minutes, or according to the package directions, until "al dente." Drain and divide among 4 shallow bowls.

- Drizzle with the pesto, then sprinkle the extra cheese over the top to serve.

---

10 **Goat Cheese, Hazelnut, and Radicchio Salad** Toast 2 tablespoons blanched hazelnuts as in the main recipe. Transfer to a cutting board and crush lightly with a rolling pin. Combine 2 tablespoons finely chopped mixed herbs in a small bowl with 1 finely chopped shallot, 1 teaspoon whole-grain mustard, 1 tablespoon sherry vinegar, 3 tablespoons olive oil, and a pinch of salt and black pepper. Arrange the leaves from 1 radicchio on 4 plates and crumble 3½ oz hard goat cheese over the salads. Sprinkle with the toasted hazelnuts and drizzle with the dressing to serve.

30 **Winter Pesto and Goat Cheese Mini Muffins** Toast 3 tablespoons hazelnuts, using 2 tablespoons to make the pesto following the main recipe. Sift 1¼ cups all-purpose flour into a bowl with 1 teaspoon baking powder and a pinch of salt. Coarsely chop or crush the reserved hazelnuts and stir into the flour with a pinch of black pepper. Break 1 egg into a small bowl, add ⅓ cup milk, ¼ cup olive oil, and 2 tablespoons of the pesto and beat together. Pour into the flour, add 3 oz finely diced hard goat cheese, and stir until barely combined. Grease 18 sections in

1 or 2 mini muffin pans or line them with paper liners. Fill with the muffin batter and bake in a preheated oven, at 375°F, for 12–15 minutes, until risen and golden. Cool a little on a wire rack and serve warm.

Warm Scallop and Radicchio Salad with Chorizo

Serves 4

1 tablespoon olive oil
4 oz chorizo sausage,
  thinly sliced
8 oz small roeless scallops
small head of radicchio,
  leaves separated
large handful of frisée
  lettuce leaves

For the dressing

1 small shallot, finely chopped
1 teaspoon Dijon mustard
2 tablespoons olive oil
2 teaspoons sherry or red
  wine vinegar
salt and black pepper

- Put the oil into a skillet, add the chorizo, and cook over medium-high heat for 2–3 minutes, until crisp. Remove with a slotted spoon and set aside.

- Return the pan to the heat and cook the scallops for 1–2 minutes, tossing them occasionally, until opaque and slightly caramelized.

- Meanwhile, whisk together the dressing ingredients.

- Arrange the salad greens on 4 plates, top with the scallops and chorizo, and drizzle with the dressing.

20 Pan-Fried Scallops with Chorizo

Cut 4 oz chorizo sausage into slices about ½ inch thick. Put 16 large roeless scallops into a bowl with 16 raw, peeled jumbo shrimp. Combine 1 teaspoon finely grated lemon zest with 2 tablespoons olive oil and ¼ teaspoon dried red pepper flakes (optional). Pour the dressing over the scallops and mix well to coat. Heat 1 tablespoon olive oil in a large skillet and cook the chorizo for about 2 minutes, until browned. Remove with a slotted spoon and set aside. Return the pan to the heat and cook the scallops and shrimp for 2–4 minutes, turning occasionally, until just cooked and starting to caramelize. Set aside and keep warm for 1–2 minutes, then serve with the salad greens and chorizo, as in the main recipe.

30 Broiled Scallop Skewers with Chorizo

Toss the chorizo and scallops from the 20-minute recipe with the dressing. Set aside to marinate for 10 minutes. Cut 8 prosciutto slices in half and wrap a scallop in each. Thread onto metal skewers, alternating them with the chorizo slices, and place on an aluminum foil-lined broiler rack. Cook under a preheated medium-hot broiler for 6–8 minutes, turning occasionally, until the scallops are opaque and the ham is crisp and golden. Serve with the salad, as in the main recipe.

30 Beet Tarte Tatin with Goat Cheese

Serves 4–6

2 tablespoons olive oil
2 garlic cloves, chopped
1 teaspoon thyme leaves
2 tablespoons balsamic vinegar
10 fresh cooked beets
  (not pickled), sliced or
  cut into thin wedges
flour, for dusting
1 sheet puff pastry, chilled
¾ cup crumbled goat cheese
thyme leaves or snipped chives,
  to garnish

- Put the oil into an ovenproof skillet over medium-low heat and, when hot, sauté the garlic and thyme for 1–2 minutes, until just softened. Pour in the vinegar and simmer gently for 1–2 minutes, until just sticky.

- Arrange the beets to fit snugly and attractively in the pan, then increase the heat slightly and cook for 4–5 minutes, until the underside begins to brown.

- Meanwhile, put the pastry onto a floured work surface and roll into a circle about ½ inch larger than the skillet.

- Lay the pastry over the skillets, tucking the edges in neatly to cover the beets, and bake in a preheated oven, at 400°F, for 15–20 minutes, until the pastry is puffed and golden.

- Invert the tart onto a large plate, then sprinkle with the goat cheese and serve garnished with the thyme or chives.

---

1 Goat Cheese and Beet Tartlets

Trim 4 small seeded or herb tortilla wraps so that they fit into a 4–section popover pan or 4 sections in a large muffin pan but overhang slightly. Place in a preheated oven, at 350°F, for 2–3 minutes, until beginning to brown. Meanwhile, combine 6 cooked and diced fresh beets (not pickled) in a bowl with ¾ cup diced or crumbled goat cheese, 1 teaspoon chopped chives, and a pinch of salt and black pepper. Spoon this mixture into the prepared pan and return to the oven for 2–3 minutes, until the cheese is beginning to melt and the tortillas are crisp and golden. Transfer to serving plates and serve drizzled with a little olive oil and some store-bought balsamic glaze, accompanied by a arugula salad.

2 Individual Goat Cheese and Beet Quiches

Unroll 1 sheet of chilled rolled dough pie crust and use to line 4 greased, individual quiche pans. Fill the pastry shells with 1¼ cups diced, cooked beet, ⅔ cup defrosted peas, and ⅔ cup crumbled goat cheese. Break 3 eggs into a small bowl, beat together, then mix in 3 tablespoons light cream and 1 teaspoon chopped thyme leaves. Pour into the filled shells and bake in a preheated oven, at 425°F, for 12–15 minutes, or until set and golden.

 # Leek and Chestnut Pancakes

Serves 4

4 tablespoons butter
2 leeks, sliced
2 cups finely sliced white
  button mushrooms
4 cooked chestnuts, crumbled
2 teaspoons chopped tarragon
1/3 cup dry hard cider or
  apple juice
1/2 cup light cream
1/3 cup all-purpose flour
2/3 cup milk
1 extra-large egg, lightly beaten
salt and black pepper
mixed salad, to serve (optional)

- Melt half the butter in a skillet and cook the leeks for 5–6 minutes, until soft and golden. Add the mushrooms, chestnuts, and tarragon and cook for another 4–5 minutes, until softened. Pour in the cider and simmer until completely evaporated. Stir in the cream, then season and simmer for 1 minute to thicken slightly. Remove from the heat and keep warm. Meanwhile, sift the flour into a bowl with a pinch of salt. Make a well in the center and pour in the milk and egg. Mix well, using a wire whisk, until the batter is smooth.

- Melt a pat of the remaining butter in a nonstick skillet or 9½ inch crepe pan over medium heat. Pour one-quarter of the batter into the pan and swirl to spread out. Cook for 1–2 minutes, until set and lightly golden underneath. Flip and cook the other side for 30–60 seconds, until golden. Transfer to a plate and keep warm. Repeat to make another 3 pancakes with the remaining batter.

- Place the pancakes on warm plates, fill with the leek and chestnut mixture, then fold and serve with a mixed salad.

1 Leek and Chestnut Soda Breads

Put ½ oz mixed, dried mushrooms into a saucepan with 1 cup boiling water. Simmer for 7–8 minutes, until softened. Drain, then coarsely chop. Meanwhile, cook the leeks as above. Add 4 cooked, chopped chestnuts and 1 teaspoon chopped tarragon and cook for another minute. Stir in ½ cup cream cheese and the mushrooms, stirring until the cheese has melted. Spoon onto toasted soda bread and serve.

2 Leek and Chestnut Phyllos

Brush 4 individual popover or quiche pans with melted butter. Brush four 12 inch square sheets of phyllo pastry with melted butter and cut each into 4 equal squares. Use these to line the prepared pans, arranging the squares at slightly different angles. Bake in a preheated oven, at 400°F, for about 8 minutes, until golden. Meanwhile, cook the creamy leek and chestnut filling by following the main recipe.

Stir 1/3 cup cream cheese into the mixture with the cream. Carefully transfer the pastry shells to plates. Spoon in the filling and serve immediately, sprinkled with grated Parmesan cheese, if desired.

10 Smoked Duck with Clementine and Walnut Salad

Serves 4

2 clementines
½ bunch of watercress,
   plus a handful of extra leaves,
   to garnish
½ cup walnuts, lightly crushed
8 oz smoked duck breast, sliced
pomegranate seeds, to garnish
   (optional)

For the dressing

2 tablespoons walnut oil
2 teaspoons raspberry vinegar
salt and black pepper

- Cut away the peel and pith from the clementines. Cut the flesh into segments, discarding the membrane, but reserving the juice in a small bowl.

- Arrange the watercress on 4 plates and sprinkle with the clementine segments and the walnuts. Top with the smoked duck slices and garnish with the watercress leaves and pomegranate seeds, if using.

- To make the dressing, whisk the oil and vinegar into the reserved clementine juice and season to taste. Drizzle the dressing over the salad and serve.

2 Warm Duck, Clementine, and Walnut Salad

Prepare the clementines and dressing following the main recipe. Place 2 tablespoons olive oil in a skillet over medium heat. Generously season 6 oz duck cutlets and sprinkle with ½ teaspoon Sichuan pepper. Put into the hot pan and cook for 3–4 minutes, turning once, until cooked but still slightly pink. Transfer to a warm place to rest for 10 minutes. Slice the duck and sprinkle it over the salads with the walnuts and pomegranate seeds from the main recipe. Serve drizzled with the dressing.

3 Sliced Duck with Clementines

Prepare the clementines as in the main recipe, reserving the juice. Remove any excess fat from 2 duck breasts, then score the flesh with a sharp knife and season with salt and black pepper. Heat a dry skillet and cook the duck breasts, skin side down, over medium-high heat, for 8–10 minutes, until really golden. Lower the heat and pour in the reserved clementine juice. Turn and cook the breasts for another 5–10 minutes, until the juices are slightly sticky and the flesh still pink. Transfer to a warm place to rest for 10 minutes, then slice thickly.

Arrange on plates with the salad greens, clementine segments, and walnuts, as in the main recipe. Serve drizzled with the warm clementine and duck juices.

30 Ricotta and Winter Herb Gnocchi

Serves 4

3 tablespoons olive oil

1 onion, chopped

3 garlic cloves, chopped

1½ cups fresh bread crumbs

1½ teaspoons grated lemon zest

3 tablespoons chopped herbs,
such as thyme, parsley,
rosemary, chives, and sage

½ cup shredded cheddar cheese
or Swiss cheese

1 (16 oz) package fresh gnocchi

⅔ cup defrosted and chopped
frozen leaf spinach

1 cup ricotta cheese

¼ cup heavy cream

¼ teaspoon ground nutmeg

salt and black pepper

- Heat 2 tablespoons of the oil in a skillet and cook the onion and 2 of the garlic cloves over medium heat for 5–6 minutes, stirring frequently, until softened.

- Meanwhile, combine the bread crumbs in a bowl with the remaining garlic and oil, ½ teaspoon of the lemon zest, half the herbs, the cheese, and seasoning. Mix well.

- Cook the gnocchi in a large saucepan of lightly salted boiling water according to package directions. Drain.

- Squeeze any excess moisture from the spinach and place in a bowl with the cooked onion and garlic, the ricotta, the remaining herbs and lemon zest, the cream, and nutmeg. Beat together, then season to taste.

- Stir the gnocchi into the ricotta mixture and divide among 4 individual, shallow ovenproof dishes. Top with the bread crumb mixture and bake in a preheated oven, at 375°F, for 15–20 minutes, or until bubbling and golden.

---

1 Golden Gnocchi with Winter Herb and Ricotta Dip

Heat 1 tablespoon oil in a skillet over medium heat. Add 1 (16 oz) package gnocchi and cook for 5–7 minutes. Meanwhile, put ⅔ cup ricotta into a bowl with 2 teaspoons chopped herbs, 1 teaspoon grated lemon zest, 2 tablespoons crème fraîche or sour cream, and salt and black pepper. Mix until smooth, then divide among 4 small dishes. Put the gnocchi into 4 pasta bowls and serve accompanied by the dishes of ricotta dip.

2 Winter Herb and Ricotta Frittata

Sauté 1 (16 oz) package gnocchi in an ovenproof saucepan following the 10-minute recipe. Meanwhile, beat 4 eggs in a bowl with ⅔ cup ricotta, 2 teaspoons chopped herbs, and a generous pinch of salt and black pepper. Pour the egg mixture over the gnocchi and cook over medium-low heat for 6–7 minutes, until just set. Meanwhile, combine 1 cup freshly made bread crumbs with 2 teaspoons chopped parsley, ½ cup shredded Emmental cheese or Swiss cheese, and 2 teaspoons olive oil. Mix well. Sprinkle ½ cup ricotta over the top of the frittata and top with the herb bread crumbs. Put the frittata under a preheated medium-hot broiler for 3–4 minutes, until golden. Serve cut into wedges.

Skier's Cheese and Bacon Tart

Serves 4

1 tablespoon olive oil
7 oz smoked bacon pieces
or pancetta
1 sheet ready-to-bake puff
pastry, chilled
1 teaspoon fine cornmeal
3 tablespoons crème fraîche
1 onion, halved and thinly sliced
¾ cup shredded Swiss cheese
½ teaspoon dried thyme
green salad, to serve (optional)

- Put the oil into a large skillet over medium heat and cook the bacon for 3–4 minutes, until cooked but not browned. Remove with a slotted spoon and drain on paper towels.

- Place the pastry onto a baking sheet lightly dusted with the cornmeal. Spread the crème fraîche over it, leaving a ½ inch border all around the edge.

- Sprinkle the onion and cheese over the crème fraîche, followed by the bacon, and finally the thyme. Bake in a preheated oven, at 425°F, for 12–15 minutes, until crisp and golden, then serve with a green salad, if desired.

Skier's Cheese on Toast

Lightly toast 4 thick slices of sourdough or country-style bread. Meanwhile, put ¼ cup crème fraîche or sour cream into a bowl and combine with ⅔ cup shredded Swiss cheese, half a finely chopped onion, and ½ teaspoon dried thyme. Top the toasted bread with a slice of cured ham, such as prosciutto, then spread the cheesy mixture thickly over the ham. Place on an aluminum foil-lined broiler rack and put under a preheated medium-hot broiler for 3–5 minutes, until melting. Serve with a small green salad.

Skier's Cheese Souffle

Melt 2 tablespoons butter in a saucepan over low heat. Mix in 3 tablespoons all-purpose flour to form a paste, then stir over the heat for 45 seconds. Remove the pan from the heat and stir in ⅔ cup milk, a little at a time, until smooth. Return the pan to the heat and cook the sauce, stirring constantly, until it thickens. Transfer to a large bowl and set aside to cool slightly. Meanwhile, whisk 2 egg whites in a large, clean bowl until they form soft peaks. Beat ½ cup cream cheese into the bowl of sauce with ¾ cup shredded Swiss cheese, ½ teaspoon dried thyme, 2 egg yolks, and 2 slices finely chopped cured ham. Gently fold the egg whites into the mixture, then spoon into 4 greased individual souffle dishes. Place on a baking sheet and bake in a preheated oven, at 400°F, for 15–18 minutes, until risen and golden. Serve immediately.

WIN-FIRE-NEX

Warm Potato and Mackerel Salad

Serves 4

12 oz new potatoes, halved
3 tablespoons olive oil
2 teaspoons red wine vinegar
1 tablespoon whole-grain mustard
1 banana shallot, finely chopped
1 tablespoon rinsed and thinly
　sliced pickle
2 teaspoons rinsed and
　drained capers
8 cherry tomatoes, halved
2 tablespoons Kalamata-style
　olives, drained
4 small mackerel fillets, boned
　and skin lightly scored
large handful of frisée leaves
salt and black pepper

- Cook the new potatoes in a large saucepan of salted boiling water for 12–15 minutes, until just tender. Drain, return to the pan and toss with 2 tablespoons of the olive oil. Add all the remaining ingredients, except the mackerel and frisée, then season to taste. Set aside.

- Heat the remaining tablespoon of olive oil in a large, nonstick skillet and cook the mackerel fillets, skin side down, for 3–4 minutes, until the flesh turns white. Gently turn them over and cook for another minute, until lightly golden. Remove from the pan and cool slightly before flaking the flesh.

- Arrange the frisée on serving plates and serve with the warm potato salad and flaked mackerel.

Quick Smoked Mackerel Pâté

Put 8 oz peppered smoked mackerel fillets into a food processor with 2 tablespoons crème fraîche or sour cream, ⅔ cup cream cheese, and 2 teaspoons lemon juice. Blend until almost smooth, then transfer to a bowl and stir in 2 tablespoons finely chopped parsley or chives. Sprinkle a few thinly sliced pickles over the top to garnish, and serve with rice cakes or freshly made toast.

Hot Smoked Mackerel and Potato Pâté

Put 2 russet or Yukon gold potatoes into a saucepan with 1½ cups hot milk, 1 chopped garlic clove, and a generous pinch of salt and black pepper. Bring to a boil, then simmer for about 15 minutes, or until the potatoes are tender. Meanwhile, prepare the mackerel pâté following the 10-minute recipe. Drain the potatoes, reserving the milk, and mash until smooth. Beat the pâté into the potatoes with 2 tablespoons olive oil and enough of the reserved milk to create a soft, spreadable mixture. Spoon into bowls, garnish with sliced pickles and chopped parsley, and serve warm with crusty bread or toast.

QuickCook
Hearty Soups and Stews

Recipes listed by cooking time

3

2

Red Pepper Soup with Spicy Caraway and Chickpea Salsa

Serves 4

1 (32 oz) carton good-quality roasted red pepper soup

2 tablespoons olive oil

½ red onion, chopped

2 garlic cloves, chopped

1 red chile, chopped (and seeded if less heat preferred)

1 (15 oz) can chickpeas, rinsed and drained

1 teaspoon caraway seeds

2 ripe but firm tomatoes, seeded and diced

2 tablespoons chopped cilantro

crusty bread, to serve

- Heat the soup in a large saucepan, according to the directions on the carton.

- Meanwhile, make the salsa. Heat the olive oil in a skillet and cook the onion, garlic, and chile over medium heat for 5–6 minutes, until slightly softened. Add the chickpeas and caraway seeds, cook for 2 minutes, then stir in the tomatoes and remove from the heat.

- Stir most of the salsa and half the cilantro into the hot soup, then ladle into bowls. Top with the remaining salsa and cilantro and serve immediately with crusty bread.

Spiced Pepper and Chickpea Stew with Caraway Seed and cut 1 yellow and 2 red bell peppers into chunks. Cut 1 red onion into chunks. Heat 2 tablespoons olive oil in a large saucepan and cook the vegetables over medium-high heat for 7–8 minutes. Reduce the heat slightly and add 2 chopped garlic cloves, 1 chopped red chile, and 1 teaspoon caraway seeds and stir for 1–2 minutes. Add 3 cups good-quality, spicy pasta sauce, 2 (15 oz) cans rinsed and drained chickpeas, and the grated zest of 1 lemon. Simmer for 7–8 minutes, then ladle into dishes. Garnish with cilantro and serve with steamed couscous, rice, or pasta.

Harissa-Spiced Pepper and Chickpea Soup Heat 2 tablespoons olive oil in a large saucepan and cook 2 diced red bell peppers and 1 chopped red onion over medium-high heat for 7–8 minutes. Reduce the heat and stir in 1–2 tablespoons harissa paste (depending on the heat desired), 2 tablespoons tomato paste, 1 teaspoon caraway seeds, and 1 teaspoon ground cumin. Stir over the heat for 1–2 minutes, then pour in 2 cups tomato puree or tomato sauce, 2 cups hot vegetable stock, and 1 (15 oz) can rinsed and drained chickpeas. Season generously, then cover and simmer gently for about 15 minutes, until the bell peppers are soft. Blend to the desired consistency, then ladle into bowls and serve drizzled with a little chili or olive oil and a sprinkling of toasted cumin seeds, if desired.

Chicken and Spinach Stew

Serves 4

1¼ lb skinless, boneless chicken thighs, thinly sliced

2 teaspoons ground cumin

1 teaspoon ground ginger

2 tablespoons olive oil

1 tablespoon tomato paste

2 (14½ oz) cans cherry tomatoes

⅓ cup raisins

1¼ cups cooked green lentils

1 teaspoon grated lemon zest

1 (5 oz) package baby spinach

salt and black pepper

freshly chopped parsley, to garnish (optional)

steamed couscous or rice, to serve (optional)

• Mix the chicken with the ground spices until well coated. Heat the olive oil in a large saucepan or Dutch oven, then add the chicken and cook for 2–3 minutes, until lightly browned.

• Stir in the tomato paste, tomatoes, raisins, lentils, and lemon zest, season, and simmer gently for about 12 minutes, until thickened slightly and the chicken is cooked.

• Add the spinach and stir until wilted. Ladle the stew into bowls, then sprinkle with parsley and serve with steamed couscous or rice, if desired.

Quick Spinach and Watercress Soup

Melt 2 tablespoons butter in a large saucepan and sauté 1 chopped garlic clove and 2 chopped scallions over medium heat for 2–3 minutes. Add 6 oz cooked, peeled new potatoes and 4 cups hot vegetable stock. Bring to a simmer, then add 1 bunch of watercress and 4 cups chopped spinach leaves. Heat for 1–2 minutes, then blend until smooth. Season, then add a pinch of ground nutmeg. Ladle into bowls and top each with a dollop of crème fraîche or Greek yogurt and a dusting of grated nutmeg.

Chicken and Rice Soup with Lemon

Heat 2 tablespoons oil in a large saucepan and cook 4 sliced scallions and 2 chopped garlic cloves over medium heat for 2–3 minutes, until softened. Add 8 oz thinly sliced, skinless, boneless chicken breast and cook for 3–4 minutes, until lightly browned all over. Add ¾ cup washed long-grain rice and stir to coat in the oil. Pour 5 cups good-quality, hot chicken or vegetable stock into the pan, season with salt and black pepper and a pinch of freshly grated nutmeg, then simmer for about 15 minutes, until the rice is tender. Stir 3 cups chopped spinach leaves into the soup and stir for 1–2 minutes, until the leaves have wilted. Ladle into bowls and serve with lemon wedges.

Quick Carrot and Cilantro Stew

Serves 4

2 tablespoons olive oil

14 carrots (about 1¾ lb), sliced

1 inch piece of fresh ginger root,
  peeled and finely chopped

2 garlic cloves, sliced

2 teaspoons baharat or ras el hanout

1 teaspoon ground coriander

pinch of saffron threads (optional)

8 dried apricots, sliced

1 preserved lemon, chopped

1¾ cups hot vegetable stock

chopped cilantro, to garnish

steamed couscous, to serve

- Heat the oil in a large saucepan or Dutch oven and cook the carrots, ginger, and garlic for 5–6 minutes, until beginning to soften. Add the spices and apricots and stir for a minute before adding the preserved lemon and hot stock. Cover and simmer for 10–12 minutes, until tender.

- Ladle the stew into bowls, sprinkle with the cilantro, and serve with couscous.

Carrot and Cilantro Soup with Cumin Toasts

Pour 2 (18 oz) cartons store-bought carrot and cilantro soup into a large saucepan and heat over medium-low heat. Meanwhile, put 3 tablespoons olive oil into a skillet, add 2 teaspoons cumin seeds, and put over medium-low heat for 2–3 minutes, until the cumin starts to brown. Toast 4 seeded pita breads, then drizzle half the cumin oil over them and cut into strips. Ladle the soup into bowls and garnish with chopped cilantro. Drizzle the remaining cumin oil on top and serve immediately with the cumin toasts.

Moroccan-Style Carrot and Cilantro Soup

Heat 2 tablespoons olive oil in a large saucepan or Dutch oven and add 1 chopped onion, 1 tablespoon peeled and chopped fresh ginger root, and 2 chopped garlic cloves. Cook over medium heat for 7–8 minutes, until softened. Stir in 1 teaspoon ras el hanout and 1 teaspoon ground coriander, then add 12 chopped carrots (about 1½ lb) and 1 chopped sweet potato. Stir to coat, then pour in 5 cups hot vegetable or chicken stock. Cover and simmer over medium heat for about 15 minutes, until the vegetables are tender. Blend the soup with a handheld blender, then season to taste and ladle into bowls. Garnish with plenty of freshly chopped cilantro to serve.

 # Quick Pea and Leek Soup

Serves 4

4 tablespoons butter

2 banana shallots, finely chopped

2 leeks, thinly sliced

1 tablespoon chopped mixed
herbs, such as sage, thyme,
chives, and parsley

½ cup crème fraîche or
Greek yogurt

4 cups good-quality boiling
vegetable stock

2⅓ cups frozen small peas

salt and black pepper

- Melt the butter in a large saucepan over medium heat, then add the shallots and leeks and cook for 5–6 minutes, until softened.

- Meanwhile, stir the chopped herbs into the crème fraîche or Greek yogurt and set aside.

- Add the vegetable stock and small peas to the leeks and simmer for 2–3 minutes, until the peas are just tender.

- Season to taste, then ladle into bowls and serve immediately with a dollop of herbed crème fraîche.

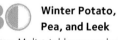

2 Potato, Pea, and Leek Soup

Heat 2 tablespoons olive oil in a large saucepan or Dutch oven and add 7 diced Yukon gold or red-skinned potatoes (about 1¾ lb), 2 chopped leeks, and 3 thinly sliced scallions. Cook over medium heat for 5 minutes, stirring frequently, until the leek is beginning to soften. Add 5 cups boiling vegetable or chicken stock, season, and simmer over medium heat for about 12 minutes, until the potatoes are tender, adding 1 cup frozen peas for the final 2–3 minutes. Blend the soup until smooth, then ladle into bowls and serve with the herbed crème fraîche, as above, if desired.

3 Winter Potato, Pea, and Leek

Stew Melt 2 tablespoons butter with 1 tablespoon olive oil in a large saucepan or Dutch oven. Add 3 thickly sliced leeks and 2 chopped garlic cloves and cook for 4–5 minutes, until beginning to soften. Meanwhile, chop 4 Yukon gold or red-skinned potatoes and 2 sweet potatoes into chunks. Add to the pan with ¼ cup pearled spelt or pearl barley, 1¾ cups boiling vegetable stock, 1 rosemary sprig, and 2 thyme sprigs. Season with a pinch of salt and plenty of black pepper, and simmer for 20–22 minutes, adding 1⅓ cups frozen peas for the final 3–4 minutes. When everything is tender, discard the herb sprigs and ladle the stew into deep dishes. Garnish with chives and serve with crusty bread.

WIN-HEAR-GUF

30 Chinese-Style Beef and Ginger Stew

Serves 4

2 tablespoons vegetable oil
1 onion, halved and sliced
1 inch piece ginger root, peeled
   and cut into matchsticks
2 garlic cloves, sliced
3 scallions, sliced diagonally
1 teaspoon Chinese five spice
½ teaspoon dried red pepper
   flakes (optional)
1 star anise
3 tablespoons oyster sauce
2 tablespoons light soy sauce
1½ tablespoons cornstarch, mixed
   with 1 tablespoon water
2½ cups beef stock
1 lb top sirloin steak, thinly sliced
3 cups shredded snow peas
steamed jasmine rice, to serve

- Heat half the oil in a large saucepan and stir-fry the onion over medium heat for 4–5 minutes, until softened. Add the ginger, garlic, and scallions, and stir-fry for 2–3 minutes, until softened slightly. Reduce the heat to low, add the spices, and cook for 1–2 minutes, until aromatic.

- Combine the oyster sauce and soy sauce, add to the cornstarch mixture, then stir into the stock and bring to a boil. Simmer for 10 minutes, stirring occasionally.

- Meanwhile, heat the remaining oil in a hot wok or skillet and stir-fry the beef over high heat for 3–4 minutes, until browned all over. Set aside.

- Add the snow peas to the stock, simmer for 2–3 minutes, then add the beef. Spoon into bowls and serve immediately with steamed jasmine rice.

10 Beef and Ginger Soupy Noodles

Heat 5 cups beef broth in a saucepan and add a 1½ inch piece fresh ginger root cut into matchsticks, 1 sliced red chile, and 2 tablespoons dark soy sauce. Simmer for 2–3 minutes, then add 1¼ lb straight-to-wok or prepared thick noodles and simmer for 2 minutes. Add 12 oz thinly sliced top sirloin steak, 2 cups shredded snow peas, and ½ cup bean sprouts and cook for 1–2 minutes, until the beef browns. Ladle into bowls and serve immediately.

20 Ginger Beef Broth with Winter

Greens Cut 1 lb top sirloin steak into thin slices, cutting against the grain. Put into a bowl with 1 tablespoon peeled and grated fresh ginger root, 1 crushed garlic clove, 1 finely chopped red chile (optional), and 1 teaspoon minced lemon grass. Mix well, then set aside to marinate for 5 minutes. Heat 2 tablespoons vegetable oil in a large saucepan or wok and stir-fry the beef for 3–4 minutes over medium-high heat, until aromatic. Add 3 cups good-quality hot beef stock, 3 tablespoons oyster sauce, and 2 tablespoons light soy sauce and simmer for 2–3 minutes. Add 5 cups shredded collard greens into the pan and simmer for 3–4 minutes, until wilted. Ladle into bowls and top each one with a small handful of bean sprouts to serve.

WIN-HEAR-BOU

20 Quick Parsnip and Lentil Dhal

Serves 4–6

1½ cups split red lentils
2 tablespoons vegetable oil
1 onion, finely chopped
2 garlic cloves, crushed
1 tablespoon peeled and grated
  fresh ginger root
2 teaspoons mild curry powder
1 teaspoon garam masala
½ teaspoon ground turmeric
4 parsnips, diced
1¾ cups hot vegetable stock
2 tablespoons coconut milk
3 cups coarsely chopped spinach
salt and black pepper
naan, to serve

- Cook the lentils in a saucepan of boiling water for, 15 minutes, or according to the package directions, until tender.

- Meanwhile, heat the vegetable oil in a large saucepan and cook the onion, garlic, and ginger for 5–6 minutes over medium heat, stirring frequently, until starting to brown. Add the spices and parsnips, cook for 1 minute, then add the stock and coconut milk and cook for about 10 minutes, until tender.

- Drain the lentils and add to the stock pan. Add the spinach and stir for 1 minute, until wilted. Season to taste, then spoon into bowls and serve with naan.

10 Lentil Soup with Spiced Parsnip

Croutons Heat 2 tablespoons vegetable oil in a large saucepan over medium-high heat and cook 1 grated red onion, 2 crushed garlic cloves, and 2 teaspoons peeled and grated fresh ginger root for 4–5 minutes, until softened. Meanwhile, heat 2 tablespoons vegetable oil in a skillet and cook 2 finely diced parsnips over medium-high heat for 7–8 minutes, turning frequently, until tender and golden. Drain on paper towels. Add the spices from the main recipe to the onion mixture and cook for 1 minute. Now add 4 cups cooked or canned green lentils and 5 cups boiling vegetable stock. Simmer for 3–4 minutes, until tender, then blend to desired consistency. Ladle into bowls and serve topped with the golden parsnip croutons.

30 Curried Parsnip and Lentil Soup

Heat 2 tablespoons oil in a large saucepan and cook 1 chopped onion, 2 chopped garlic cloves, and 1 tablespoon peeled and grated fresh ginger root for 4–5 minutes over medium-high heat until starting to brown. Reduce the heat, then stir in the spices from the main recipe, ⅔ cup red lentils, and 7 chopped parsnips (about 1¾ lb). Cook for 1 minute, then add 5½ cups hot vegetable stock and 1 cup coconut milk. Cover and simmer for 15 minutes. Blend, season, and serve with naan.

 # Lamb and Gnocchi Casserole

Serves 4

3 tablespoons olive oil
1 lb boneless lamb, cubed
1 onion, chopped
2 garlic cloves, chopped
1 bay leaf
1 tablespoon chopped fresh
   oregano, plus extra to serve
2 tablespoons tomato paste
½ cup red wine
2 (14½ oz) cans cherry tomatoes
   or diced tomatoes
1 teaspoon grated lemon zest
1 (16 oz) package fresh
   potato gnocchi
½ cup crumbled feta cheese
salt

- Heat 2 tablespoons of oil in a large, flameproof skillet or casserole over high heat and cook the lamb for 2–3 minutes, until browned all over. Transfer to a plate and set aside.

- Reduce the heat slightly, then sauté the onion and garlic over medium heat for 3–4 minutes, until beginning to soften. Add the bay leaf, oregano, and tomato paste and stir over the heat for 1 minute. Pour in the red wine, boil for 1 minute, then add the tomatoes and lemon zest and simmer for 5–6 minutes, until slightly thickened. Return the lamb to the pan and simmer for 5–6 minutes, until just cooked.

- Meanwhile, cook the gnocchi in a saucepan of salted boiling water for 1–2 minutes, or according to the package directions. Drain. Arrange the gnocchi on top of the lamb mixture. Sprinkle with the feta, then drizzle with the remaining oil. Put under a preheated, medium-hot broiler for 4–5 minutes, until golden. Garnish with extra oregano leaves.

 Lamb Ratatouille with Golden Gnocchi Heat 2 tablespoons oil in a skillet and brown 4 lamb leg cutlets over high heat for 1 minute on each side. Add ½ cup red wine and simmer to reduce by half. Add 3 cups prepared ratatouille, then simmer for 3–5 minutes, until the lamb is cooked. Meanwhile, heat 1 tablespoon oil in a skillet and sauté 1 (16 oz) package fresh potato gnocchi over medium heat for 3–5 minutes. Serve with the ratatouille, topped with oregano and crumbled feta, if desired.

Baked Lamb Gnocchi Cook 1 (16 oz) package fresh potato gnocchi in a large saucepan of boiling salted water for 1–2 minutes, or according to the package directions, then drain. Meanwhile, heat 2 tablespoons olive oil in a large, flameproof skillet or Dutch oven and brown 4 thick lamb cutlets for 1 minute on each side. Add 3 cups prepared ratatouille and 1 (15 oz) can rinsed and drained great Northern beans (optional) and bring to a boil. Top with an even layer of the gnocchi, then sprinkle with ½ cup crumbled feta cheese and 1 teaspoon dried oregano. Drizzle with 1 tablespoon olive oil, then transfer the pan to a preheated oven, at 400°F, for 12–15 minutes, until the gnocchi is golden. Remove and serve with a Greek-style salad.

20 Jerk Chicken and Sweet Potato Soup

Serves 4–6

2 tablespoons vegetable oil
1 red onion, chopped
1 celery stick, chopped
1 inch piece of fresh ginger root, peeled and chopped
1 tablespoon jerk seasoning
6 sweet potatoes (about 2 lb), chopped (or a mixture of sweet potatoes and butternut squash)
5 cups hot chicken stock
2 tablespoons lime juice
2 cups shredded cooked chicken
salt and black pepper
thinly sliced scallions, to garnish

- Heat the vegetable oil in a large saucepan and sauté the onion, celery, and ginger for 4–5 minutes, until beginning to soften. Add the jerk seasoning, then mix in the sweet potatoes and stir over the heat for 1 minute.

- Pour the chicken stock into the pan and simmer over medium heat for about 12 minutes, until the potatoes are tender. Blend to the desired consistency, then stir in the lime juice and season to taste.

- Ladle the soup into bowls and top each with a handful of the shredded chicken. Garnish with scallions and serve.

---

10 Quick Jerk Chicken Broth

Heat 2 tablespoons oil in a large saucepan over medium heat, and add 3 sliced scallions along with 1 tablespoon peeled and grated ginger root. Cook for 1–2 minutes, until softened. Stir in 1 tablespoon jerk spice mix and cook for 1 minute before pouring in 5 cups hot chicken stock. Simmer for 3–4 minutes, then remove from the heat and stir in 2 cups shredded, cooked chicken and 1–2 tablespoons lime juice. Ladle into bowls and serve, garnished with extra sliced scallions, if desired.

30 Jerk Chicken and Sweet Potato

Curry Coat 1 lb diced chicken thighs in 1½ tablespoons jerk spice mix or paste and set aside. Heat 2 tablespoons vegetable oil in a large saucepan over medium-high heat and sauté 1 chopped onion, 1 large chopped red bell pepper, 2 chopped garlic cloves, and 2 teaspoons peeled and chopped fresh ginger root for 6–7 minutes, until softened. Add the chicken to the pan and stir frequently for 2–3 minutes, until browned all over. Add 4 chopped sweet potatoes and stir to coat. Pour in 2 cups hot chicken stock and simmer gently over medium heat for 12–15 minutes, until the chicken is cooked and the sweet potatoes are tender. Serve spooned over rice, garnished with sliced scallions.

WIN-HEAR-DUA

30 Spicy Black-Eyed Peas and Sausages

Serves 4

6 thick, Italian-style spicy sausages

1 tablespoon olive oil

8 oz chorizo, cubed

2 leeks, thickly sliced

1 celery stick, finely sliced

2 garlic cloves, chopped

½ cup dry white wine

1¾ cups hot chicken stock
or vegetable stock

2 teaspoons freshly chopped sage

1 tablespoon whole-grain mustard

1 (15 oz) can black-eyed peas,
rinsed and drained

crusty bread, to serve (optional)

- Broil the sausages under a preheated hot broiler for 5–6 minutes, turning occasionally, until browned. Set aside to cool slightly.

- Meanwhile, heat the oil in a large saucepan or Dutch oven and add the chorizo, leeks, and celery. Cook over medium heat for 4–5 minutes, until slightly softened. Add the garlic and cook for another 2 minutes. Pour the wine into the pan and boil to reduce by half. Add the stock, sage, mustard, and beans and return to a boil.

- Once the sausages are cool enough to handle, slice them. Add to the saucepan and simmer gently for 15 minutes, until cooked through and the sauce has thickened slightly.

- Spoon into dishes and serve with plenty of crusty bread.

---

10 Black-Eyed Pea Soup with Sizzled Sausages

Melt 4 tablespoons butter in a saucepan and cook 2 chopped leeks and 1 chopped celery stick over medium heat for 4–5 minutes. Meanwhile, remove the casings from 3 spicy sausages. Heat 1 tablespoon oil in a skillet and cook the sausages over high heat, breaking them up as they cook, until crisp and golden. Add 2 chopped garlic cloves to the leek mixture, heat for 2 minutes, then add 2 (15 oz) cans rinsed and drained black-eyed peas and 5 cups hot vegetable stock. Bring to a boil, then blend. Ladle the soup into bowls and serve topped with the sausagemeat.

20 Sausage and Black-Eyed Pea Soup

Broil 6 spicy Italian-style sausages under a medium-hot broiler for 12–14 minutes, turning occasionally, until cooked and golden. Meanwhile, melt 4 tablespoons butter in a large saucepan and cook 2 thinly sliced leeks and 2 finely chopped celery sticks over medium heat for 5–6 minutes, until beginning to soften. Add 2 chopped garlic cloves and cook for another 2 minutes. Pour ½ cup dry white wine into the pan and boil to completely evaporate. Add 1 (15 oz) can rinsed and drained black-eyed peas, 1 tablespoon chopped sage, and 4 cups hot stock and simmer for 7–8 minutes, until everything is tender. Slice the sausages thickly and divide among 4 bowls. Ladle over the soup and serve, garnished with freshly chopped parsley.

 # Coconut Fish Laksa with Lemon Grass

Serves 4

3 tablespoons laksa paste or
  Thai red curry paste)
1¾ cups coconut milk
1¾ cups hot vegetable stock
2 teaspoons Thai fish sauce
2 lemon grass stalks, finely sliced
  (woody outer leaves discarded)
8 oz ribbon rice noodles
1¼ lb white fish fillet chunks,
  any bones removed
1½ cups bean sprouts

To garnish (optional)
cilantro leaves
1 sliced red chile

- Place the laksa paste and coconut milk in a large saucepan and bring to a boil. Simmer for 2–3 minutes, then add the stock, fish sauce, and lemon grass and simmer for another 5 minutes.

- Meanwhile, prepare the rice noodles according to the package directions, until tender.

- Stir the chunks of fish into the soup and continue to simmer gently for 3–4 minutes, until cooked. Add the bean sprouts and remove from the heat.

- Drain the noodles and pile into bowls. Ladle the soup over the noodles and serve the laksa garnished with cilantro leaves and sliced red chile, if desired.

---

10 Quick Shrimp and Coconut Soupy

Noodles Put 2 tablespoons laksa or Thai red curry paste into a hot saucepan with 1¾ cups coconut milk, 1 teaspoon lemon grass paste, 4 cups vegetable stock, and 2 tablespoons Thai fish sauce. Bring to a boil and simmer for 4–5 minutes. Add 10 oz cooked, peeled shrimp and 12 oz rice noodles, cooked. Simmer for 2 minutes, until the noodles are soft and the shrimp hot. Ladle the soupy noodles into bowls and serve garnished as above, if desired.

30 Eastern Coconut Fish Stew

Heat 2 tablespoons vegetable oil in a large saucepan and cook 3 sliced banana shallots for 3–4 minutes, until softened and lightly browned. Add 2 crushed garlic cloves, 2 teaspoons peeled and finely grated fresh ginger root, and 2 finely chopped lemon grass hearts and stir-fry for another 2 minutes. Add 3 tablespoons laksa paste or Thai red curry paste and 3 tablespoons coconut milk and cook over medium heat for 2–3 minutes. Add another 1½ cups coconut milk plus 1¼ cups chicken or fish stock and 2 shredded lime leaves or the finely grated zest of 1 lime. Bring to a boil, then simmer for about 10 minutes. Cut 12 oz chunky, boneless white fish fillets into bite-size pieces and add to the pan with 8 oz raw, peeled jumbo shrimp. Simmer for 3–4 minutes, until cooked through. Serve with glutinous rice and garnished as above, if desired.

 Chicken and Rice Soup in a Mug

Serves 4–6

2 tablespoons vegetable oil

1 onion, coarsely grated

1 garlic clove, crushed

3 tablespoons medium-hot
curry paste

½ teaspoon ground turmeric

4 cups hot chicken stock

1 small apple, peeled and grated

4 cups cooked long-grain rice

3 cups cooked bite-size
chicken pieces

3 cups small croutons

chopped cilantro, to garnish

- Heat the oil in a large saucepan and cook the onion and garlic for 3–4 minutes over medium-high heat, stirring frequently, until softened.

- Add the curry paste and turmeric, stir for 1 minute, then add the stock, apple, and rice. Simmer for 3–4 minutes to thicken slightly.

- Stir in the chicken, then ladle the soup into wide mugs. Top with the croutons and the cilantro.

Quick Chicken and Rice Soup

Heat 2 tablespoons oil in a large saucepan and add 1 chopped onion, 2 chopped garlic cloves, 1 chopped carrot, and 2 chopped potatoes. Cook over medium heat for 6–7 minutes, stirring frequently. Stir in 2 tablespoons mild curry paste and cook for 1 minute. Add 5 cups hot chicken stock and 1 small, peeled and grated apple. Bring to a boil and simmer for 8–10 minutes, until tender. Blend to desired consistency, or leave chunky, then stir in 2 cups cooked long-grain rice and 2 cups shredded cooked chicken. Ladle into bowls and serve garnished with croutons and cilantro, if desired.

Chicken and Rice Stew

Heat 2 tablespoons vegetable oil in a large saucepan and cook 1 coarsely chopped onion and 1 red bell pepper for 5–6 minutes, until beginning to soften. Add 2 crushed garlic cloves and 2 teaspoons peeled and grated fresh ginger root and cook for another minute. Add 3 tablespoons mild paste and cook for anoother 1 minute. Cut 1 lb boneless, skinless chicken thighs into bite-size pieces and add to the pan along with ½ cup split red lentils. Cook for 2–3 minutes, stirring frequently, until the chicken browns. Pour in 2 cups boiling chicken stock, then add 1 small, peeled and grated apple and 2 diced potatoes. Bring to a boil and cook for 15–18 minutes, until the vegetables and lentils are tender. Serve with steamed long-grain rice and garnish with chopped cilantro.

30 Lazy Winter Vegetable Stew

Serves 4–6

1½ lb new potatoes, peeled
2 tablespoons butter
1 onion, chopped
2 garlic cloves, chopped
2 cups good-quality, boiling
　vegetable or lamb stock
3 parsnips, cut into chunks
1 small celeriac, peeled and
　cut into chunks
3 carrots, sliced ½ inch thick
2 leeks, thickly sliced
1 tablespoon chopped rosemary
2 tablespoons olive oil
salt and black pepper
finely chopped curly parsley,
　to garnish (optional)

- Cook the potatoes in a large saucepan of salted boiling water for 8–10 minutes, until just tender. Drain well and set aside to cool slightly.

- Meanwhile, melt the butter in a large saucepan or Dutch oven and cook the onion and garlic over medium heat for about 5 minutes, until slightly softened and browned.

- Pour in the stock and add the prepared vegetables and rosemary. Season with a pinch of salt and black pepper, then cover and simmer over medium heat for 15–20 minutes, until the vegetables are tender.

- Once the potatoes are cool enough to handle, slice thickly. Heat the oil in a large, nonstick skillet and sauté the potatoes over medium heat for 10–12 minutes, turning occasionally, until crisp and golden. Drain on paper towels.

- Ladle the vegetable stew into shallow bowls, top with the potato slices, and serve immediately, garnished with freshly chopped parsley, if desired.

10 Cream of Vegetable Soup

Bring 5 cups good-quality vegetable stock to a boil with 1 rosemary sprig. Add 2 lb mixed frozen vegetables plus a pinch of salt and black pepper and simmer for 5–6 minutes, until the vegetables are tender. Discard the rosemary and blend the soup to desired consistency, adding a little extra liquid, if necessary. Ladle into bowls, drizzle 1 tablespoon light cream over each, and add a small pinch freshly grated nutmeg to serve.

20 Winter Vegetable Soup

Heat 4 tablespoons butter in a large saucepan and cook 2 chopped leeks over medium heat for 3–4 minutes, until beginning to soften. Add 2 lb mixed, finely chopped winter vegetables, such as squash, potatoes, carrots, and parsnips (the chopping can be done in a food processor, if you prefer). Cook for another 2–3 minutes. Add 5 cups boiling vegetable stock, season with a pinch of salt and black pepper, then cover and simmer rapidly for 10–12 minutes, or until the vegetables are just tender. Blend to desired consistency, adding more liquid, if necessary, then ladle into deep bowls. Serve immediately, drizzled with rosemary oil or olive oil and sprinkled with grated pecorino cheese.

3⦿ Peperonata-Style Pork and Chorizo Casserole

Serves 4

2 tablespoons olive oil
1 lb pork tenderloin, cubed
4 oz chorizo sausage, diced
1 red bell pepper, seeded and sliced
1 onion, halved and sliced
2 garlic cloves, chopped
2 cups button mushrooms, sliced
1 tablespoon sweet smoked paprika
4 red-skinned or white round
  potatoes, cubed
1 (14½ oz) can diced tomatoes
¾ cup hot vegetable stock
2 tablespoons chopped parsley
salt and black pepper
boiled long-grain rice, to serve
½ cup sour cream, to serve

- Heat the olive oil in a large, deep skillet and brown the pork over medium-high heat for 2–3 minutes, turning occasionally. Add the chorizo, cook for 1 minute, then transfer all the meat to a plate and set aside.

- Cook the bell pepper and onion in the skillet for 3–4 minutes, until beginning to soften. Add the garlic and mushrooms and cook for another 2–3 minutes, until slightly softened.

- Stir in the paprika and potatoes and heat for 1 minute. Add the tomatoes and stock and simmer for about 12 minutes, until the potato is almost tender.

- Return the meat to the pan and cook for another 5–6 minutes, until the pork is cooked but still juicy. Season to taste.

- Sprinkle the goulash with chopped parsley. Serve in dishes with cooked long-grain rice and dollops of sour cream.

1⦿ **Chunky Chorizo and Peperonata on Rice** Heat 2 tablespoons olive oil in a large skillet and cook 12 oz pork strips over medium-high heat for 2–3 minutes, until browned. Add 8 oz diced chorizo and cook for 1–2 minutes, until golden, then add 2 cups quartered mushrooms and cook for 2–3 minutes, until softened. Drain 1 (7 oz) jar sliced, mixed roasted peppers, add to the pan, and stir to heat through. Serve immediately with rice, sour cream, and a sprinkling of chopped parsley.

2⦿ **Chorizo Peperonata with Pork** Put 3 tablespoons olive oil into a large skillet over medium heat and sauté 2 sliced red bell peppers, 1 sliced yellow or orange bell pepper, and 1 sliced red onion for 3–4 minutes. Reduce the heat slightly and add 3 oz thinly shredded sliced chorizo, 1 teaspoon chopped thyme, and a generous pinch of salt and black pepper. Cook for another 10 minutes, stirring occasionally, adding 2 thinly sliced garlic cloves for the final 3–4 minutes. When everything is softened and lightly browned, stir in 2 ripe diced tomatoes and 2 teaspoons sherry or balsamic vinegar and heat for another 1–2 minutes, until the tomatoes begin to collapse. Meanwhile, heat 2 tablespoons olive oil in a large skillet and cook 4 seasoned pork chops for about 10 minutes, turning once, until cooked through but still juicy. Place on 4 warm plates and serve with the chorizo peperonata.

Quick Mushroom and Garlic Tom Yum

Serves 4

1 tablespoon tom yum paste
  (sold in Asian grocery stores)
4 cups vegetable stock
5 oz oyster mushrooms, sliced
7 oz closed-cup mushrooms,
  sliced
3½ oz enoki mushrooms
  (optional)
2 scallions, thinly sliced
2 garlic cloves, sliced
1 inch piece fresh ginger root,
  peeled and sliced
lime juice, to serve

- Put the tom yum paste into a large saucepan with the stock and bring to a simmer. Add the mushrooms, scallions, garlic, and ginger and simmer for 5–6 minutes, until the flavors develop and the mushrooms soften.

- Ladle into bowls and serve immediately with a squeeze of lime juice.

20 Wild Mushroom and Garlic Broth

Put 1 oz mixed dried mushrooms into a saucepan with 4 cups just simmering water. Cover and cook for 10 minutes, until softened. Meanwhile, heat 2 tablespoons oil in a saucepan and sauté 1 diced celery stick, 1 sliced leek, 2 chopped shallots, and 2 chopped garlic cloves over medium heat for 7–8 minutes, until softened. Add 10 oz sliced portobello mushrooms and cook for another 2 minutes, until just beginning to soften. Strain the dried mushrooms, reserving the liquid, then slice and add to the vegetables. Stir, then add the reserved mushroom stock and simmer for 4–5 minutes. Ladle into bowls and serve.

30 Roasted Garlic Mushroom Soup

Arrange 1¼ lb portobello mushrooms, stem side up, in a shallow ovenproof dish. Put 4 tablespoons softened butter into a bowl with 1 small crushed garlic clove, 2 tablespoons chopped parsley, and a pinch of salt and black pepper. Mash together with a fork, then smear over the mushrooms. Roast in a preheated oven, at 400°F, for about 15 minutes, until softened and aromatic. Meanwhile, melt 2 tablespoons butter in a large saucepan with 1 tablespoon olive oil and sauté 1 chopped celery stick, 1 chopped potato, 1 sliced leek, and 2 teaspoons freshly chopped thyme leaves over medium-low heat, stirring occasionally, for 10–12 minutes, until softened. Pour in 3⅓ cups hot beef or vegetable stock, increase the heat slightly, and simmer for another 5–6 minutes, until the vegetables are tender. Remove the roasted mushrooms from the oven, add to the pan, and simmer for 2–3 minutes. Blend the soup to the desired texture, then ladle into bowls and serve with crusty bread.

WIN-HEAR-TIG

30 Jumbo Shrimp and Sweet Potato Curry

Serves 4

2 tablespoons vegetable oil
1 large onion, chopped
2 garlic cloves, sliced
1 tablespoon peeled and chopped
　fresh ginger root
1 green chile, thinly sliced
3 tablespoons mild curry paste
2 sweet potatoes, diced
1¾ cups coconut milk
1 cup vegetable stock
small handful of curry leaves
12 oz jumbo shrimp
⅔ cup defrosted and drained
　frozen spinach

To serve

steamed pilaf rice or naan
cilantro leaves, freshly chopped

- Heat the oil in a large, deep skillet or wok and sauté the onion over medium-high heat for 3–4 minutes, until beginning to brown. Add the garlic, ginger, and chile and stir-fry for another 2 minutes. Reduce the heat slightly and add the curry paste, stirring for 1–2 minutes.

- Add the sweet potato dice, tossing them to coat, then add the coconut milk, stock, and curry leaves. Simmer gently for 12–15 minutes, until the sweet potato is almost tender.

- Add the shrimp and spinach and stir over the heat for 2–3 minutes, until the shrimp are just cooked through.

- Spoon the curry into dishes, and serve immediately with steamed pilaf rice or naan and chopped cilantro.

1 Curried Shrimp Broth

Heat 2 tablespoons oil in a large saucepan and sauté 2 sliced banana shallots and 2 sliced garlic cloves over high heat, stirring, for 2–3 minutes. Reduce the heat, add 1 tablespoon mild curry paste, and stir for 1 minute. Pour 4 cups hot vegetable stock into the pan. Add 10 oz peeled jumbo shrimp, 2 cups cooked long-grain rice, 2 seeded and diced tomatoes, and 2 tablespoons chopped cilantro. Simmer for 2–3 minutes, then ladle into bowls to serve.

2 Quick Shrimp Curry

Heat 2 tablespoons oil in a large skillet and sauté 1 finely sliced onion, 2 sliced garlic cloves, and 1 tablespoon peeled and chopped fresh ginger root over medium-high heat for 3–4 minutes, until beginning to soften. Stir in 2 tablespoons mild curry paste and cook for 1 minute before adding 1 (14½ oz) can diced tomatoes and 1 cup water. Simmer for about 12 minutes, until thickened slightly, then add 1 lb peeled jumbo shrimp. Simmer for another 2–3 minutes, until the shrimp are cooked. Serve with a dollop of plain yogurt and chopped cilantro.

WIN-HEAR-MYF

Italian Beans with Pancetta

Serves 4

3 tablespoons extra virgin olive oil, plus extra to drizzle
10 oz pancetta, cubed
3 banana shallots, chopped
2 teaspoons chopped thyme
2 (15 oz) cans cranberry beans, rinsed and drained
1 (15 oz) can cannellini beans, rinsed and drained
1 cup vegetable stock
salt and black pepper

To serve (optional)
crusty bread
Parmesan cheese, grated
parsley, freshly chopped

- Heat the oil in a heavy skillet and sauté the pancetta over high heat for 2–3 minutes, until golden. Reduce the heat slightly, add the shallots and thyme, and cook for another 2–3 minutes, stirring occasionally, until just softened.

- Add the beans and vegetable stock, season with a pinch of salt and plenty of pepper, and simmer over medium heat for 2–3 minutes, until tender.

- Spoon into bowls, drizzle with a little extra olive oil, and serve immediately with crusty bread, plenty of Parmesan, and parsley, if desired.

2 **Italian Minestrone Soup with Pancetta** Heat 2 tablespoons oil in a saucepan over medium heat and cook 2 chopped shallots, 2 chopped garlic cloves, 1 chopped celery stick, and 1 chopped carrot for 5–6 minutes, stirring. Add 1 (14½ oz) can diced tomatoes, 1 (15 oz) can rinsed and drained cranberry beans, and 4 cups hot vegetable stock. Simmer for 10–12 minutes, adding 4 oz mini pasta shapes for the final 5 minutes. Meanwhile, sauté 8 oz cubed pancetta over medium-high heat for 5–6 minutes. Ladle the soup into bowls, sprinkle with the pancetta, and serve as above.

3 **Chunky Italian Stew with Pancetta** Heat 2 tablespoons olive oil in a large saucepan or Dutch oven over medium-high heat and add 8 oz cubed pancetta, 1 chopped onion, 2 chopped garlic cloves, 2 sliced celery sticks, and 2 diced carrots. Cook for 5–6 minutes, until beginning to brown. Add 2 diced potatoes, 1 (14½ oz) can plum tomatoes, coarsely chopped, 1 (15 oz) can rinsed and drained cannellini or cranberry beans, 1 teaspoon dried oregano, and 3 cups hot vegetable or chicken stock. Season generously and simmer over medium heat for about 15 minutes before adding 2 oz macaroni or other small pasta. Cook for another 5–6 minutes, or according to package directions, until the pasta and vegetables are tender. Serve ladled into shallow bowls, as above.

WIN-HEAR-TEH

Spiced Tomato and Chorizo Soup

Serves 4

3 tablespoons olive oil
1 red onion, chopped
2 garlic cloves, chopped
1 teaspoon hot smoked paprika
2 (15 oz) cans lima beans, chopped
1 cup drained sun-dried tomatoes
2 cups tomato puree or tomato sauce
3¾ cups vegetable stock
5 oz chorizo, diced
salt and black pepper
chopped parsley, to garnish
crusty bread, to serve

- Heat 2 tablespoons of the oil in a large saucepan or Dutch oven and sauté the onion and garlic over medium heat for 4–5 minutes, until slightly softened.

- Add the paprika and lima beans and stir for 1 minute before adding the sun-dried tomatoes, tomato puree or sauce, and stock. Bring to a boil, then simmer for about 10 minutes, until thickened slightly.

- Meanwhile, heat the remaining oil in a small skillet and cook the chorizo for 2–3 minutes, stirring frequently, until golden. Drain on paper towels and set aside.

- Blend the soup to the desired consistency, then season to taste and ladle into bowls. Top with the chorizo and parsley and serve immediately with plenty of crusty bread.

Spicy Tomato and Lima Bean Bowl

Heat 2 tablespoons oil in a skillet over medium heat and cook 8 oz cubed chorizo sausage for 2–3 minutes. Reduce the heat slightly and add 1 chopped red chile or 1 teaspoon dried red pepper flakes and 1 chopped garlic clove. Cook for 1–2 minutes, until just softened. Add 2 (15 oz) cans rinsed and drained lima beans and 4 diced ripe tomatoes. Stir gently for 2–3 minutes, until warmed through, then season. Add 2 tablespoons chopped flat leaf parsley and 2 teaspoons sherry vinegar, stir again, and serve immediately with peppery arugula leaves, if desired.

Spicy Tomato and Chorizo Casserole

Heat 1 tablespoon olive oil in a large saucepan or Dutch oven over medium heat. Cut 8 oz spicy chorizo sausage into chunks and cook for 2–3 minutes, stirring occasionally, until golden. Add 1 large sliced red onion and 2 chopped garlic cloves and sauté for 4–5 minutes, until softened. Stir in 1 teaspoon hot smoked paprika, then add 3⅓ cups peeled, seeded, and diced butternut squash and heat for 1 minute. Add 2 cups tomato puree or tomato sauce, ⅔ cup vegetable stock or water, 1 large drained and sliced roasted pepper (optional), and 1 (15 oz) can rinsed and drained chickpeas or lima beans. Bring to a boil and season with salt and black pepper, then cover and simmer for about 15 minutes, until the casserole is rich and thick and the squash is tender. Ladle into bowls and garnish with plenty of freshly chopped flat leaf parsley.

WIN-HEAR-DAR

30 Cowboy Beef and Bean Casserole

Serves 4

2 tablespoons olive oil

1 onion, chopped

2 garlic cloves, chopped

1 lb top sirloin steak, cut into strips

1½ tablespoons chipotle paste

1 teaspoon ground cumin

1½ teaspoons sweet smoked
  paprika

6 oz smoked pork sausage,
  thickly sliced

1 cup lager

1 (14½ oz) can diced tomatoes

2 tablespoons tomato paste

1 (15 oz) can kidney or navy
  beans, rinsed and drained

1 roasted red pepper, drained
  and sliced (optional)

Tabasco or other hot sauce

salt and black pepper

To serve

baked potatoes or steamed rice

sour cream (optional)

- Heat the oil in a large saucepan or Dutch oven. Add the onion and garlic and sauté for 6–7 minutes, stirring frequently, to soften.

- Meanwhile, toss the beef strips in the chipotle paste, cumin, and paprika. Add the beef and sausage to the onion mixture and stir over medium heat for 1 minute. Add the lager, tomatoes, tomato paste, beans, red pepper (if using), and a few shakes of Tabasco. Season with salt and black pepper, then cover and simmer over medium-low heat for about 20 minutes, or until rich and thick.

- Ladle into dishes and serve with baked potatoes or steamed rice and a dollop of sour cream, if desired.

---

10 Cowboy Bean Stew

Heat 2 tablespoons oil in a skillet over medium-high heat. Mix 1½ lb top sirloin steak strips with the chipotle paste and spices, as above, and stir-fry for 5–6 minutes, until the meat is browned. Add 2 (15 oz) cans baked beans, heated, 1 tablespoon Worcestershire sauce, and a few shakes of Tabasco. Serve as above.

20 Cowboy Beef and Bean Soup

Heat 2 tablespoons olive oil in a large saucepan or Dutch oven and cook 1 finely chopped onion, 1 finely chopped celery stick, and 1 chopped garlic clove over medium heat for 3–4 minutes, until beginning to soften. Increase the heat and add 12 oz ground round or ground sirloin beef, stirring frequently for 3–4 minutes, until browned all over. Add 2 tablespoons tomato paste and stir constantly for 1 minute. Pour in 4 cups hot beef stock plus 1 (15 oz) can rinsed and drained pinto or black beans and a few shakes of Tabasco. Simmer over medium heat for about 10 minutes to let the flavors develop. Ladle into bowls and serve immediately.

WIN-HEAR-KAO

# Soupy Butternut Squash and Ham Rice Bowl

Serves 4

1 butternut squash, peeled, seeded, and cut into ½ inch cubes

2 tablespoons sweet chili sauce

2 scallions, finely sliced

2 teaspoons peeled and chopped fresh ginger root

5 cups boiling good-quality ham or vegetable stock

8 oz piece cooked ham, shredded or diced

2 cups cooked rice

salt and black pepper

chopped cilantro, to garnish (optional)

- Put the squash, chili sauce, scallions, and ginger into a large saucepan, add the stock, and cook for about 8 minutes, until the squash is just tender.

- Add the ham and rice to the pan for the final 2 minutes. Season to taste and ladle into bowls and serve garnished with the cilantro, if desired.

Ham and Butternut Squash Soup

Put 2 tablespoons olive oil into a large saucepan over medium-low heat and cook 2 teaspoons peeled and finely chopped fresh ginger root, ½–1 teaspoon dried red pepper flakes (depending on heat desired), and 2 chopped garlic cloves for about 2 minutes, until softened. Add 1 peeled, seeded, and diced butternut squash and 5 cups hot vegetable stock and simmer for 12–15 minutes, until the squash is tender. Add 8 oz cooked ham, diced, and blend the soup to the desired consistency. Ladle into bowls to serve.

Torn Ham and Butternut Squash Casserole

Put 2 tablespoons olive oil in a large saucepan or Dutch oven over medium heat and sauté 1 sliced red onion for 5–6 minutes, until beginning to soften. Add 2 chopped garlic cloves, 2 teaspoons peeled and chopped fresh ginger root, ½–1 teaspoon dried red pepper flakes (depending on heat desired), and 1 teaspoon cumin seeds. Cook for another 2 minutes, then add 1 peeled and seeded butternut squash cut into chunks. Add 2 cups vegetable stock and half a cinnamon stick, and simmer for 12–15 minutes, until thick and tender. Stir 2 cups cooked pearl barley or other grain into the casserole along with 8 oz cooked ham, torn into pieces. Bring back to a simmer, season with black pepper, and ladle into dishes.

Bean, Bacon, and Cabbage Soup with Rosemary Pistou

Serves 4

¼ cup olive oil
8 oz thick bacon, chopped
1 onion, chopped
1 celery stick, sliced
1 carrot, diced
4 cups ham stock
1 bay leaf
1 (15 oz) can cannellini or navy
  beans, rinsed and drained
2 tablespoons chopped rosemary
1 small garlic clove, crushed
½ small head of savoy cabbage,
  shredded
salt and black pepper
Parmesan cheese, grated,
  to serve

- Heat 1 tablespoon of the oil in a large saucepan or Dutch oven and cook the bacon for 2–3 minutes over medium-high heat to brown. Add the onion, celery, and carrot, reduce the heat slightly, and cook for 5–6 minutes, stirring occasionally, until slightly softened.

- Add the stock and bay leaf and bring to a boil. Add the beans and simmer for 10–12 minutes, until the vegetables are almost tender.

- Meanwhile, using a small food processor or a mortar and pestle, grind the rosemary with the remaining 3 tablespoons of oil, the garlic, and a pinch of salt and black pepper.

- Add the cabbage to the soup and simmer for another 3–5 minutes, until just tender. Season to taste, then ladle into bowls and serve hot, drizzled with a little rosemary pistou and a sprinkling of Parmesan.

---

10 Wilted Winter Greens with Bacon and Pesto Heat 2 tablespoons oil in a large saucepan and cook 8 oz chopped bacon for about 3–4 minutes, until golden. Add 2 crushed garlic cloves, cook for 1 minute, then pour in 2 cups hot ham stock and 2 tablespoons pesto. Return to a boil, then stir in 6 cups shredded winter greens (such as kale, Swiss chard, savoy cabbage, or spinach) or collard greens. Simmer for 3–4 minutes, until just tender, then ladle into bowls and serve with extra pesto, if desired.

20 Winter Greens Soup with Pistou Melt 2 tablespoons butter with 2 tablespoons olive oil in a large saucepan and cook 1 chopped onion, 1 chopped potato, and 2 thinly sliced leeks over medium heat for 5–6 minutes, until beginning to soften. Meanwhile, prepare the pistou sauce as in the main recipe. Pour 4 cups boiling vegetable or ham stock into the onion mixture, then cover and simmer for 7–8 minutes, until the vegetables are almost tender. Add 4 cups shredded winter greens or collard greens and cook for 3–4 minutes, until everything is tender. Blend the soup to the desired consistency, then ladle into bowls and serve drizzled with the pistou, as above.

10 Thai Chicken Noodle Broth

Serves 4

1 tablespoon vegetable oil

2 tablespoons green Thai curry paste

4 cups good-quality clear chicken broth

1 tablespoon Thai fish sauce

1 teaspoon sugar

1 sliced red chile (optional)

2–3 kaffir lime leaves, shredded (optional)

8 oz thin rice noodles

2 cups shredded, cooked chicken

thinly sliced scallions, to garnish (optional)

- Heat the oil in a large saucepan and cook the curry paste for 1 minute over medium-low heat, until aromatic. Pour in the chicken stock, then add the fish sauce, sugar, chile, and lime leaves, if using. Bring to a boil and simmer for 4–5 minutes to let the flavors to develop.

- Meanwhile, bring a large saucepan of water to a boil. Add the noodles, then turn off the heat and set aside for 3 minutes, until tender. Alternatively, cook according to the package directions. Drain well, then divide the noodles among 4 bowls. Top with the shredded chicken, then ladle the hot broth over the top. Garnish with scallions to serve, if desired.

---

20 Winter Thai Chicken Soup

Heat 2 tablespoons oil in a large saucepan and cook 2 sliced banana shallots for 2–3 minutes, until beginning to soften. Add 4 cups mixed chopped sweet potato and butternut squash and 2 tablespoons Thai red curry paste. Cook for 1 minute over medium-low heat, then pour in 2½ cups hot chicken stock and 1¾ cups coconut milk with the Thai fish sauce, sugar, chile, and lime leaves from the main recipe. Simmer for 12–15 minutes, until tender. Stir in 2 cups cooked, shredded chicken, then ladle the soup into bowls to serve.

30 Winter Thai Chicken Curry

Heat 2 tablespoons vegetable oil in a large saucepan and cook 2 sliced banana shallots for 2–3 minutes, until beginning to soften. Add 1 lb boneless, skinless chicken thighs to the pan and cook for 3–4 minutes, stirring occasionally, until the meat browns. Stir in 4 cups of mixed diced winter vegetables, such as butternut squash, celeriac, parsnip, and sweet potato. Add 2 tablespoons green Thai curry paste and stir for 1–2 minutes, until the chicken and vegetables are coated and aromatic. Pour in 1¾ cups coconut milk and 1 cup chicken stock, plus the Thai fish sauce, sugar, red chile, and lime leaves from the main recipe. Simmer gently for about 15 minutes, until the vegetables are tender. Serve with steamed Thai rice.

WIN-HEAR-ZUX

Quick Sausage and Mushroom Stew

Serves 4

2 tablespoons olive oil

2 garlic cloves, sliced

2 scallions, sliced

8 oz cremini mushrooms, halved

3 cups tomato-base pasta sauce

7 oz small, cooked link sausages, halved, or Italian-style cooked link sausages, quartered

To serve

Parmesan cheese, grated

Crusty bread

- Heat the olive oil in a deep skillet and sauté the garlic and scallions over medium heat for 1 minute, until slightly softened. Add the mushrooms and cook for about 5 minutes, stirring occasionally, until soft and golden.

- Add the pasta sauce and sausages and stir over the heat for 2–3 minutes, until hot. Serve immediately with plenty of crusty bread and grated Parmesan.

Sausage Stew with Mushrooms

Broil 8 Italian-style link sausages under a preheated medium-hot broiler for 12 minutes, turning occasionally, until cooked through. Meanwhile, heat 2 tablespoons oil in a saucepan, add 1 sliced onion and 2 chopped garlic cloves, and sauté for 4–5 minutes. Add 8 oz halved mushrooms and cook for another 4–5 minutes. Pour in 3 cups tomato-based pasta sauce and simmer for 2–3 minutes. Once the sausages are cool enough to handle, slice diagonally and add to the pan. Cook, stirring, for another 2 minutes, then serve with crispy fried potatoes and freshly grated Parmesan.

Farmhouse Sausage and Mushroom Gratin

Broil the sausages and prepare the mushroom stew following the 20-minute recipe, then place the sausages in a shallow ovenproof dish. Meanwhile, put 1½ cups freshly made coarse bread crumbs into a bowl and stir in 2 tablespoons olive oil, 2 finely chopped scallions, 2 tablespoons freshly grated Parmesan, 1 tablespoon finely chopped mixed herbs (such as parsley, rosemary, and thyme), and a pinch of salt and black pepper. Cover the sausages with the mushroom stew and stir lightly to combine. Sprinkle the crumble mixture evenly over the top and place in a preheated oven, at 400°F, for 12–15 minutes, until crisp and lightly golden. Serve with a green salad.

WIN-HEAR-XAS

10 Hearty Pea and Lentil Soup with Crispy Cured Ham

Serves 4

4 tablespoons butter

3 scallions, sliced

1 garlic clove, crushed

2½ cups hot ham stock or vegetable stock

1 (15 oz) can chickpeas, rinsed and drained

2 cups cooked green lentils or canned green lentils in water, rinsed and drained

1⅓ cups frozen peas

3 sage leaves, chopped (optional)

1 tablespoon olive oil

4 slices prosciutto

salt and black pepper

- Melt the butter in a large saucepan and cook the scallions and garlic over medium heat for 1–2 minutes, until softened.

- Add the stock, chickpeas, lentils, peas, and sage, if using. Simmer for 5–6 minutes, until the peas are tender.

- Meanwhile, heat the oil in a large skillet and sauté the prosciutto until crispy, turning once. Drain on paper towels.

- Blend the soup to the desired consistency, season to taste, then ladle into bowls and crumble some of the ham on top.

20 Ham and Lentil Peasouper

Melt 4 tablespoons butter in a large saucepan and add 1 chopped onion, 1 chopped celery stick, 2 chopped garlic cloves, and 2 chopped potatoes. Cook over medium-low heat for 10 minutes, stirring frequently, until softened. Add 5 cups hot ham stock, 2 cups cooked green lentils or drained, canned green lentils, 8 oz piece of ham, chopped, and 1⅓ cups frozen peas. Bring to a boil and simmer for 5–6 minutes, until the peas are soft. Blend to the desired consistency, then ladle into bowls and serve garnished with crumbled crispy bacon.

30 Chunky Ham and Lentil Stew

Melt 4 tablespoons butter in a large saucepan or Dutch oven and add 2 thickly sliced leeks, 1 sliced celery stick, 2 diced carrots, 1 chopped onion, 2 chopped garlic cloves, and 2 potatoes cut into chunks. Cook over medium-low heat for 12–15 minutes, until softened and lightly browned. Add 2 cups cooked green lentils or drained, canned green lentils and 12 oz cooked, pulled ham hock (if unavailable, cut or tear the meat from a piece of ham into bite-size pieces). Pour in 2 cups hot ham or vegetable stock, add 2 thyme sprigs and 1 bay leaf, and simmer over medium heat for about 10 minutes, until the vegetables are tender. Serve ladled into bowls with freshly cooked peas and crusty bread.

Mexican Beef Chili Soup

Serves 4

2 tablespoons vegetable oil
1 red bell pepper, cut into strips
1 red onion, halved and thinly sliced
1 red chile, thinly sliced
1½ teaspoons ground cumin
2 tablespoons tomato paste
4 cups hot beef stock
1 (15 oz) can black beans or kidney
  beans, rinsed and drained
1 cup frozen or canned corn
  kernels, drained if necessary
12 oz thick top sirloin steak
2 tablespoons lime juice
cilantro leaves, to garnish

To serve (optional)
tortilla chips
grated cheese

- Heat 1 tablespoon of the oil in a large saucepan and cook the bell pepper and onion over medium-high heat for 4–5 minutes, until lightly browned. Reduce the heat, add the chile, cumin, and tomato paste, and stir for 1 minute.

- Add the stock, beans, and corn kernels, then simmer for 5–6 minutes to let the flavors develop.

- Meanwhile, heat the remaining tablespoon oil in a skillet and cook the steak for 1–2 minutes each side, depending on the pinkness desired. Transfer to a plate and let rest for 2–3 minutes. Slice the steak into strips, cutting against the grain, and pour any juices from it into the soup.

- Ladle the soup into bowls, add the beef and lime juice, garnish with cilantro, and serve immediately, accompanied by tortilla chips and grated cheese, if desired.

---

10 Mexican Red Pepper and Meatball Bowl Heat 2 tablespoons oil in a saucepan and sauté 1 sliced red bell pepper and 1 sliced red onion over medium-high heat for 5–6 minutes. Reduce the heat, then add 12 oz cooked meatballs plus 2 teaspoons Mexican spice blend and stir for 1 minute. Pour in 2 cups Mexican cooking sauce and bring to a boil. Simmer for 1–2 minutes. Spoon into bowls, garnish with cilantro and serve with tortilla chips and grated cheese, or with steamed rice.

---

30 Mexican Meatball Stew Heat 2 tablespoons vegetable oil in a large, deep skillet and add 1 lb store-bought meatballs. Or remove the casings from 8 spicy Italian-style link sausages and form into 20–24 meatballs. Cook over medium-high heat, shaking the pan frequently, for 6–7 minutes, until the meatballs are browned all over. Transfer to a plate and set aside. Add 1 sliced red bell pepper, 1 sliced yellow bell pepper, and 1 sliced red onion to the pan, and cook over high heat for 3–4 minutes, until lightly charred. Reduce the heat slightly, add 1 tablespoon Mexican-style spice blend, and stir for 1 minute. Return the meatballs to the pan with 3 cups tomato puree or tomato sauce, 1 (15 oz) can rinsed and drained kidney beans, and 1 cup canned or frozen corn kernels (optional). Simmer over medium heat for about 15 minutes, until the meatballs are cooked and the sauce is rich and thick. Serve in bowls, garnished with cilantro leaves and accompanied by cooked rice, sour cream, and grated cheese.

QuickCook

Winter
Cold
Busters

Recipes listed by cooking time

30

20

Smoked Salmon and Edamame Cups

Serves 4

2 cups frozen edamame
(soybeans)

8 oz smoked salmon, thinly sliced

¼ cucumber, seeded and cut
into matchsticks

1 red chile, seeded and sliced

2 tablespoons sweet soy sauce

2 tablespoons coarsely chopped
cilantro leaves (optional)

3–4 small butterhead lettuce

2 teaspoons sesame seeds

- Cook the beans in a large saucepan of salted, boiling water for 2–3 minutes, or according to the package directions, until just tender. Drain and cool under cold running water.

- Meanwhile, combine the salmon, cucumber, chile, soy sauce, and cilantro in a bowl. Add the beans and toss gently to combine. Separate the lettuce leaves.

- Spoon the bean mixture into the lettuce leaves and sprinkle the sesame seeds over the top. Serve immediately.

Seared Salmon with Quinoa, Lentil, and Edamame Salad

Rub 2 tablespoons teriyaki sauce over 4 boneless salmon fillets. Heat 1 tablespoon peanut oil in a nonstick skillet and sear the salmon over medium-high heat for 2–3 minutes on each side. Transfer to a plate, cover with aluminum foil, and set aside to rest. Meanwhile, cook 2 cups frozen edamame (soybeans) as in the main recipe. Put 1¼ cups cooked green lentils and 1½ cups each of cooked red quinoa and cooked white quinoa in a bowl. Add one-quarter of a seeded and diced cucumber, 1 seeded and finely chopped red chile, 2 finely sliced scallions, and 2 tablespoons chopped cilantro. Make a dressing by combining 2 tablespoons sweet soy sauce with 3 tablespoons lime juice and 1 tablespoon sesame oil. Stir half into the quinoa mixture along with the cooled edamame, then divide the salad among 4 serving dishes. Top with the seared salmon fillets, sprinkle with 1 teaspoon sesame seeds, and drizzle with the remaining dressing, if desired.

Roasted Salmon with Quinoa and Edamame

Combine ¼ cup teriyaki marinade with 1 tablespoon sesame oil and rub over 4 boneless salmon fillets. Marinate in a small roasting pan for 10 minutes. Bring 1¾ cups vegetable stock to a boil in a saucepan, add 1 cup quinoa, and cook for 12–15 minutes. Drain. Meanwhile, sprinkle 2 teaspoons sesame seeds over the salmon fillets and place in a preheated oven, at 400°F, for 12–15 minutes, until just cooked through. Cook 2 cups frozen edamame (soybeans) as in the main recipe and stir them into the quinoa. Pile onto plates, top with the salmon, and serve with cucumber ribbons and dressing from the 20-minute recipe.

Crunchy Beef Wraps

Serves 2

1 tablespoon vegetable oil
1 (8 oz) sirloin steak
¼ cup chunky peanut butter
1 red chile, seeded and chopped
1 tablespoon dark soy sauce
1 teaspoon finely grated lime zest
1½ cups mixture of bean sprouts,
   and snow peas and carrots cut
   into matchsticks
2 large, soft plain tortilla wraps
1 tablespoon chopped cilantro
2 teaspoons lime juice
salt and black pepper

- Heat the oil in a skillet over high heat and cook the steak for 2–3 minutes on each side, until nicely browned but still medium-rare. Transfer to a plate and set aside to rest.

- Meanwhile, put the peanut butter in a small bowl, add the chile, soy sauce, and lime zest, and whisk well.

- Spread the peanut butter mixture over the tortillas, then top with the mixed vegetables and cilantro.

- Slice the steak thinly against the grain and arrange it over the vegetables. Drizzle with the lime juice, season with a pinch of salt and black pepper, then roll up tightly to serve.

---

2 **Sizzling Beef and Snow Peas**

Stir-Fry Heat 1 tablespoon oil in a wok and cook 8 oz thinly sliced top sirloin steak over high heat for 2–3 minutes. Transfer the meat to a plate and set aside. Add another tablespoon of oil to the wok and stir-fry 1 sliced garlic clove, 2 teaspoons peeled and chopped fresh ginger root, 1 chopped red chile, 2 cups shredded snow peas, and 1 sliced red bell pepper over high heat for 3–4 minutes. Return the beef to the pan with a handful of bean sprouts and toss for another minute. Add 2 tablespoons soy sauce, 2 teaspoons sesame oil, and 1 tablespoon lime juice and cook for a final minute. Serve with rice and sprinkle with crushed peanuts.

3 **Marinated Beef Skewers with Snow Peas and Noodles**

Slice 8 oz thick top sirloin steak into long, thin strips. Put into a dish with 1 tablespoon soy sauce, 1 teaspoon finely grated lime zest, and 2 teaspoons sesame oil. Mix well. Set aside to marinate for 10 minutes, then thread onto 4 metal skewers. Place 1 tablespoon oil in a large skillet and cook the beef skewers over medium-high heat for 4–5 minutes, turning occasionally, until just cooked. Transfer to a plate, cover with aluminum foil, and keep warm. Meanwhile, return the pan to the heat and stir-fry the garlic, ginger, chile, snow peas, and red bell pepper, following the

10-minute recipe. Add 10 oz straight-to-wok-style or cooked rice noodles plus 1 tablespoon light soy sauce, 1 teaspoon sesame oil, and 1 tablespoon lime juice. Toss well and heat until hot. Pile into serving dishes, top with the beef skewers and their juices, and sprinkle with chopped cilantro and crushed peanuts to serve.

Feed-a-Cold Chicken Soup

Serves 4

5 cups hot chicken stock or
   vegetable stock
1 bay leaf
1 lb boneless, skinless chicken
   thighs, trimmed of fat
2 tablespoons butter
1 celery stick, thinly sliced
2 leeks, thinly sliced
2 carrots, thinly sliced
2 cups sliced button mushrooms
1 garlic clove, chopped
½ cup frozen corn kernels
4 oz angel hair pasta
salt and black pepper
chili oil, to drizzle (optional)
chopped parsley, to garnish

- Bring the stock and bay leaf to a boil in a saucepan and add the chicken. Cover loosely and simmer for 20 minutes, until cooked and tender. Scoop out the meat with a slotted spoon and set aside to cool slightly, reserving the stock.

- Meanwhile, melt the butter in a large saucepan and cook the celery, leeks, and carrots for 7–8 minutes, until softened. Add the mushrooms and garlic and cook for another 3–4 minutes.

- Pour in the reserved stock, add the corn, and return to a boil. Season to taste. Transfer the pasta to the pan and cook for 3–4 minutes, or until "al dente."

- Shred the chicken and add to the broth. Ladle into deep bowls and serve drizzled with chili oil, if desired, and garnished with chopped parsley and black pepper.

10 **Instant Goodness Chicken Noodle Broth** Heat 4 cups chicken stock in a large saucepan with 2 teaspoons peeled and chopped fresh ginger root, 1 sliced garlic clove, 1 seeded and sliced red chile, ½ cup corn kernels, 2 cups sliced cremini mushrooms, and 1 tablespoon soy sauce. Simmer for 7–8 minutes, then add 2 cups shredded, cooked chicken breast. Meanwhile, cook 8 oz medium egg noodles according to the package directions. Pile into 4 bowls, ladle the broth over them, and serve immediately, garnished with thinly sliced scallions.

 Quick Creamy Chicken and Corn Chowder Melt 4 tablespoons butter in a large saucepan over medium heat and cook 2 chopped leeks, 1 sliced celery stick, and 1 chopped garlic clove for 3–4 minutes, until beginning to soften. Pour 4 cups milk into a separate pan with 1 teaspoon chopped thyme, 2 cloves, and 1 bay leaf and heat to boiling point. Meanwhile, add 3 finely diced Yukon gold or red-skinned potatoes to the vegetables with 3 cups diced mushrooms. Sprinkle in 1 tablespoon all-purpose flour, then season generously and stir over the heat for 1 minute. Stir the hot flavored milk into the pan and simmer for 8–10 minutes, until the potato is almost tender. Add 3½ cups diced chicken breast and 1 cup corn kernels and simmer for 2–3 minutes, until the chicken is cooked. Stir ¾ cup shredded sharp cheddar cheese (optional) into the chowder, then season to taste and serve ladled into bowls with plenty of crusty bread.

Smoked Mackerel Salad with Orange and Avocado

Serves 4

4 peppered smoked mackerel fillets, skin removed

2 small oranges

2 tablespoons avocado oil

1 (8 oz) mixed salad greens

2 firm avocados, peeled, pitted and sliced

½ cup walnut halves (optional)

salt and black pepper

- Flake the smoked mackerel fillets.

- Using a sharp knife, cut the top and bottom off each orange. Slice away the skin and pith, then cut into segments, slicing on each side of the membrane. Squeeze out the membrane before discarding it, then pour all the juice into a bowl.

- Put 3 tablespoons of the reserved juice into another bowl, add the avocado oil, salt, and black pepper, and whisk together.

- Combine the salad greens gently with the flaked mackerel, orange segments, and avocado, and arrange attractively on serving plates. Sprinkle with the walnuts, if using, then drizzle the dressing over the salad to serve.

---

2 Broiled Mackerel with Orange and Avocado Salsa

Rub 1 tablespoon olive oil over 8 small, boneless mackerel fillets, then season with salt and black pepper. Arrange, skin side up, on an aluminum foil-lined broiler rack and put under a preheated medium-hot broiler for 4–5 minutes. Turn carefully and cook for another 1–2 minutes, until the flesh turns white. Remove from the heat, cover loosely with foil, and set aside to rest. Meanwhile, cut 2 small oranges into segments, following the directions in the main recipe and reserving the juice. Dice the flesh neatly and put into a bowl with 2 small peeled, pitted, and diced avocados. Drizzle with 2 tablespoons avocado oil, 2 tablespoons of the orange juice, and 1 teaspoon red wine vinegar. Add 1 teaspoon chopped dill, season to taste, then toss gently and serve with the broiled mackerel fillets and a mixed green salad.

3 Orangey Marinated Mackerel with Avocado

Put 1 teaspoon grated orange zest in a bowl with 1 tablespoon orange juice, 2 tablespoons avocado oil, 1 tablespoon whole-grain mustard, 1 teaspoon honey, 2 tablespoons chopped parsley, and 1 teaspoon chopped dill. Season and mix well. Cut 3–4 slits in each side of 4 whole scaled, gutted, and cleaned mackerel and put the fish side by side into an ovenproof dish. Cover with the prepared marinade, massaging it into the slits, and place in a preheated oven, at 400°F, for 20–22 minutes. Serve with steamed new potatoes and an avocado and arugula salad.

Broiled Lamb with Kale and Spicy Tomato Salsa

Serves 4

1 teaspoon dried oregano
2 tablespoons olive oil
1 teaspoon grated lemon zest
4 lamb cutlets
4 cups coarsely sliced curly kale
salt and black pepper

For the salsa

2 large ripe tomatoes,
   seeded and diced
½ small red onion, finely chopped
1 large red chile, finely chopped
pinch of sugar
2 teaspoons lemon juice
1 tablespoon olive oil
2 tablespoons chopped parsley

- Combine the oregano, olive oil, and lemon zest in a bowl with a pinch of salt and black pepper, and rub the mixture all over the lamb cutlets. Arrange on an aluminum foil-lined broiler rack and put under a preheated hot broiler for 6–8 minutes, turning once, until cooked to your preference.

- Meanwhile, cook the kale in a large saucepan of salted boiling water for 5–6 minutes, until tender.

- Combine the salsa ingredients in a bowl and season to taste.

- Pile the kale onto serving plates, then arrange the lamb on top and serve with the salsa.

20 Spiced Lamb and Tomato Skewers

Put 12 oz diced lamb into a large bowl with ½–1 teaspoon dried red pepper flakes plus the oregano, olive oil, lemon zest, and seasoning from the main recipe. Add 16 red and yellow cherry tomatoes and 1 red onion cut into bite-size pieces. Mix to coat, then thread onto 4 metal skewers and arrange on an aluminum foil-lined broiler rack. Put under a preheated medium-hot broiler for 8–12 minutes, turning occasionally. Arrange on serving plates with the kale and salsa from the main recipe.

30 Spicy Lamb and Tomato

Orecchiette Heat 2 tablespoons oil in a large skillet and cook 1 chopped onion, 2 chopped garlic cloves, and 1 seeded and chopped red chile over medium heat for 6–7 minutes, stirring frequently, until softened. Increase the heat slightly and add 12 oz ground lamb and cook for 3–4 minutes, stirring occasionally, until browned. Pour in 2 cups tomato puree or tomato sauce, then add 1 tablespoon tomato paste, 1 teaspoon finely grated lemon zest, 1 teaspoon dried oregano, a pinch of sugar, and a generous pinch of salt and black pepper. Bring to a boil, then simmer, loosely covered, for about 15 minutes, adding 1½ cups shredded kale for the final 7–8 minutes. Meanwhile, cook 12 oz orecchiette pasta in a large saucepan of salted boiling water for about 10 minutes, or according to the package directions, until "al dente." Drain and serve with the spicy lamb, garnished with chopped oregano or parsley, if desired.

Crispy Salmon Ramen

Serves 2

2 teaspoons peanut oil
2 boneless salmon fillets, skin on
2 cups hot clear chicken broth
1 tablespoon lime juice
2 teaspoons Thai fish sauce
1 tablespoon soy sauce
¾ inch piece of fresh ginger root, peeled and cut into matchsticks
1 small red chile, thinly sliced
2 heads of bok choy, sliced in half lengthwise
5 oz ramen or egg noodles
cilantro leaves, to garnish

- Put the oil into a large skillet over medium heat and sauté the salmon fillets, skin side down, for 3–5 minutes, until the skin is crispy. Turn carefully and cook for another minute, until still slightly rare. Transfer to a plate and keep warm.

- Pour the stock into a saucepan, add the lime juice, fish sauce, soy sauce, and ginger, and bring to a boil. Simmer for 3–4 minutes, then add the chile and bok choy and simmer for another 4–5 minutes, until tender.

- Meanwhile, cook the noodles in a saucepan of boiling water for 2–3 minutes, or according to the package directions, until just tender. Drain and pile into bowls.

- Ladle the hot broth over the noodles and top each bowl with a salmon fillet. Serve immediately, garnished with cilantro.

10 Crispy Salmon with Noodles

Cook the salmon fillets following the main recipe. Meanwhile, heat 8 oz straight-to-wok Chinese egg noodles following the package directions. Put 1 tablespoon vegetable oil into a large wok or skillet over medium-high heat. Add 2 chopped garlic cloves, 2 teaspoons peeled and chopped fresh ginger root, 2 sliced scallions, and 1 thinly sliced red chile. Stir-fry for 2–3 minutes, then add a large handful of bean sprouts for another 1–2 minutes, until softened slightly. Add the noodles plus 1 tablespoon lime juice, 1 tablespoon soy sauce, and 1 teaspoon sesame seeds. Pile the noodle mixture into bowls, top with the salmon, and serve immediately, garnished with cilantro.

30 Steamed Salmon with Chile and Ginger

Arrange 2 boneless salmon fillets on a sheet of aluminum foil and top with the lime juice, Thai fish sauce, soy sauce, ginger, and chile from the main recipe. Scrunch together the side of the foil to enclose the fish. Put into a steamer over a saucepan of barely simmering water for about 12 minutes, until the salmon is aromatic and almost cooked. Serve with steamed bok choy and rice, garnished with sesame seeds and cilantro.

WIN-WINT-ROO

30 Chinese-Style Roasted Brussels Sprouts

Serves 2

16 Brussels sprouts
1 tablespoon vegetable oil
1 garlic clove, crushed
2 teaspoons peeled and finely
   grated fresh ginger root
2 tablespoons light soy sauce
1 teaspoon sesame oil
1½ tablespoons honey
2 tablespoons orange juice
1 star anise
large handful of bean sprouts
toasted sesame seeds, to garnish

- Trim the Brussels sprouts, cut any large ones in half through the stem, then transfer them into a roasting pan and toss with the oil. Roast in a preheated oven, at 400°F, for 20–25 minutes, until softened and browned. Meanwhile, combine the garlic, ginger, soy sauce, sesame oil, honey, orange juice, and star anise in a small saucepan and put over medium-low heat. Simmer for 4–5 minutes, stirring occasionally. Set aside and keep warm.

- Transfer the Brussels sprouts to a serving dish, add the bean sprouts and warm sauce, and toss together. Serve sprinkled with toasted sesame seeds.

10 Shredded Brussels Sprout and Cabbage Salad with Ginger Dressing

Prepare 8 oz instant thin rice noodles according to package directions. Slice 10 trimmed Brussels sprouts. Thinly shred ¼ head savoy cabbage. Put 2 tablespoons oil into a skillet and stir-fry the Brussels sprouts and cabbage over medium-high heat for 3–4 minutes. Meanwhile, whisk 1 teaspoon peeled and grated fresh ginger root with 1 tablespoon orange juice, 2 teaspoons honey, 2 tablespoons soy sauce, and 2 teaspoons sesame oil. Drain the noodles, then toss with the sprouts and cabbage, 2 teaspoons toasted sesame seeds, and the dressing. Pile into bowls and serve.

20 Chinese-Style Brussels Sprout and Ginger Stir-Fry

Put 2 tablespoons soy sauce in a bowl with 3 tablespoons freshly squeezed orange juice, 2 teaspoons sesame oil, and 1 teaspoon Chinese five spice powder. Cut 12 trimmed Brussels sprouts into quarters, through the stem. Place 1 tablespoon vegetable oil in a large wok or skillet over medium-high heat, add 2 sliced garlic cloves, a 1 inch piece of peeled and finely shredded fresh ginger root, and 1 seeded and sliced red chile. Stir-fry for 30 seconds, then add the Brussels sprouts and stir-fry for 3–4 minutes, until beginning to brown. Stir in ¼ head finely shredded savoy cabbage and cook for 2 minutes, until softened but still with some bite. Reduce the heat to low, then add the prepared sauce, stirring well. Pile the mixture into bowls and serve with steamed rice sprinkled with toasted sesame seeds.

10 Poached Smoked Haddock with Fried Eggs

Serves 4

2½ cups milk
1 bay leaf
small thyme sprig
pinch of salt
¼ teaspoon cracked mixed
 peppercorns, plus extra to serve
4 smoked haddock or cod fillets
2 tablespoons olive oil
4 eggs
5 cups cooked, chilled
 mashed potatoes

- Pour the milk into a deep skillet. Add the bay, thyme, salt, and black peppercorns and bring to simmering point.

- Add the haddock fillets and simmer gently for about 5–6 minutes, until the flesh turns opaque.

- Meanwhile, heat the oil in a large skillet and fry the eggs for about 3 minutes, or until cooked to your preference.

- Heat the mashed potatoes until warmed through and spoon onto 4 plates. Top with the poached haddock, fried eggs, and black pepper to serve.

20 Pan-Fried Haddock Fillet with Mashed Potatoes and Poached Egg

Cook 6 diced red-skinned potatoes in a saucepan of salted boiling water for 12–15 minutes. Dust 4 boneless haddock or cod fillets with seasoned flour; shake off the excess. Heat 2 tablespoons oil in a skillet and cook the fish for 6–8 minutes, turning once. Meanwhile, bring a saucepan of water to a simmer. Stir the water to create a whirlpool and break an egg into the middle of it. Poach for 3 minutes, then remove with a slotted spoon and drain on paper towels. Poach 3 more eggs in the same way. Drain the potatoes and return to the pan with 4 tablespoons butter, ¼ cup milk, and salt and black pepper. Mash until smooth, then serve with the haddock and eggs.

30 Roasted Haddock with Crispy Potatoes and Poached Eggs

Put 1 lb halved new potatoes into a roasting pan and add 1½ tablespoons olive oil, 1 teaspoon dried thyme, 2 unpeeled garlic cloves, and a generous pinch of salt and black pepper. Toss well, then roast in a preheated oven, at 425°F, for 20–25 minutes, turning occasionally, until the potatoes are crisp and tender. Meanwhile, heat 1 tablespoon olive oil in a large, flameproof skillet. Add 4 pieces chunky haddock or cod fillets and cook over medium-high heat, skin side down, for 2–3 minutes, until the skin is crispy. Drizzle with ½ tablespoon olive oil, season with coarsely ground mixed peppercorns and a small pinch of salt, and transfer the pan to the oven for 8–10 minutes, until the fish is just cooked and flaky. Meanwhile, poach the eggs as in the 20-minute recipe. Serve with the crispy potatoes and roasted fish.

 Roasted Squash and
Chickpea Stew

Serves 4

½ butternut squash, peeled,
   seeded, and cut into chunks
3 tablespoons olive oil
1 red onion, cut into thin wedges
2 garlic cloves, chopped
¾ inch ginger root, chopped
2 teaspoons ras el hanout
1 zucchini, cut into chunks
1 (15 oz) can chickpeas
1 (15 oz) can diced tomatoes
2 teaspoons honey
½ cup vegetable stock
salt and black pepper

To garnish

chopped cilantro
toasted slivered almonds

- Put the squash into a roasting pan, add 1 tablespoon of the olive oil, and season generously with salt and black pepper. Toss well, then roast in a preheated oven, at 425°F, for 20–25 minutes, turning occasionally, until tender.

- Meanwhile, heat the remaining oil in a large saucepan or Dutch oven and sauté the onion, garlic, and ginger over medium heat for 5–6 minutes. Stir in the ras el hanout and zucchini, cook for 1 minute, then add the chickpeas, tomatoes, honey, and stock. Stir to combine and simmer gently for 15–18 minutes, until thickened and tender.

- Stir the roasted squash into the tomato mixture, garnish with the cilantro and almonds, and serve immediately.

---

1   **Stew-Spiced Chickpeas with Preserved Lemon** Heat 2 tablespoons olive oil in a large skillet and cook 1 chopped red onion, 2 chopped garlic cloves, and 2 teaspoons peeled and finely chopped fresh ginger root for 5–6 minutes, until softened. Stir 2 teaspoons ras el hanout spice blend into the pan with ½ teaspoon sweet paprika and 1 (15 oz) can rinsed and drained chickpeas. Stir over medium heat for 1 minute, then add 3 diced ripe tomatoes, ½ small diced preserved lemon, and 2 tablespoons chopped cilantro and stir for 2 minutes, until the tomatoes start to collapse. Serve immediately with steamed couscous.

2   **Quick Vegetable and Chickpea Stew** Cook the red onion, garlic, and ginger as in the 10-minute recipe, then add 2 teaspoons ras el hanout, ½ teaspoon turmeric, 1 teaspoon sweet paprika, and a pinch of saffron. Cook for 1 minute, then stir in 2 zucchini, cubed, 2 cups cauliflower florets, ⅓ cup chopped apricots, 1 (14½ oz) can tomatoes, ½ cup hot vegetable stock, and 1 (15 oz) can rinsed, drained chickpeas. Season and bring to a boil. Cover and simmer for 10–12 minutes.

 # Mussel and Leek Carbonara

Serves 4

2 tablespoons olive oil
8 oz bacon, chopped
1 garlic clove, chopped
2 leeks, split lengthwise
    and thinly sliced
10 oz cooked shelled mussels
1½ lb fresh spaghetti
2 eggs
⅔ cup light cream
black pepper

- Put the oil into a large skillet and cook the bacon over medium-high heat for 2–3 minutes, until golden. Reduce the heat slightly, add the garlic and leeks, and cook for 4–5 minutes, stirring occasionally, until softened and golden. Add the mussels for the final 1–2 minutes, and stir until hot.

- Meanwhile, cook the spaghetti in a large saucepan of salted boiling water for 3–4 minutes, or according to the package directions, until tender.

- Put the eggs and cream into a bowl with plenty of black pepper and beat together.

- Drain the pasta and toss quickly with the mussel mixture and creamy eggs until well coated. Pile into bowls and serve immediately.

 ### Mussel, Leek, and Potato Gratin

Cook 4 thinly sliced red-skinned potatoes in a saucepan of lightly salted boiling water for 8–10 minutes, until tender. Meanwhile, prepare the mussel and leek sauce as in the main recipe but omit the eggs. Drain the potatoes and combine gently with the prepared sauce and ¾ cup shredded cheddar or Swiss cheese. Transfer to an ovenproof dish, top with another ¾ cup shredded cheese, and put under a preheated medium-hot broiler for 4–5 minutes, until bubbling and golden. Serve with plenty of green salad.

Fennel, Leek, and Mussel Risotto

Heat 2 tablespoons olive oil in a large saucepan over medium-high heat. Cook 4 oz chopped bacon for 2–3 minutes, until lightly golden. Reduce the heat slightly, add 1 small, finely chopped fennel bulb and 2 finely sliced leeks, and cook for 4–5 minutes, to soften. Stir 2 cups risotto rice into the pan for 1 minute, until the grains are coated and become slightly translucent. Pour in ½ cup dry white wine and simmer rapidly, stirring constantly until the wine has evaporated. Add 5 cups boiling fish stock or vegetable stock, a small ladleful at a time, stirring constantly at a gentle simmer until each ladleful has been absorbed. When the rice is "al dente" (after about 17 minutes), stir in 10 oz cooked shelled mussels plus 3 tablespoons crème fraîche or heavy cream. Remove from the heat, cover, and set aside to rest for 1–2 minutes before serving.

Quick Lamb and Spinach Tikka

Serves 4

2 tablespoons vegetable oil

1 lb boneless, lean lamb cutlet, cut into strips

1 onion, thickly sliced

2 garlic cloves, sliced

2 teaspoons peeled and finely grated fresh ginger root

1 teaspoon cumin seeds

1 large green chile, finely sliced (seeded if less heat desired)

2 tablespoons tikka curry paste

3 large ripe tomatoes, coarsely chopped

½ cup hot lamb stock or vegetable stock

3 cups coarsely chopped spinach

flatbreads, to serve

chopped cilantro, to garnish

- Put half the oil in a large skillet over high heat and cook the lamb, stirring, for 2–3 minutes, until browned. Using a slotted spoon, transfer to a plate and set aside.

- Return the pan to a medium-high heat and cook the onion, garlic, ginger, cumin seeds, and chile in the remaining oil for 3–4 minutes, until lightly browned. Reduce the heat slightly, then add the tikka paste, stirring for 1 minute.

- Add the tomatoes and stock and simmer for 5–6 minutes, until the sauce has thickened slightly. Stir in the spinach and heat for another 1–2 minutes, until wilted.

- Return the lamb to the pan, stir until reheated, then serve sprinkled with cilantro and with flatbreads on the side.

---

10 Curried Lamb Cutlets

Rub 2 tablespoons tandoori curry paste over 4 lamb cutlets. Put them onto an aluminum foil-lined broiler rack, put under a preheated medium-hot broiler, and cook for 6–8 minutes, turning once, until lightly charred and cooked to your preference. Set aside, covered with foil, and rest for 1–2 minutes. Serve with steamed brown rice or chapattis, a tomato and onion salad, and a tray of Indian-style pickles.

30 Lamb and Potato Madras

Heat 2 tablespoons vegetable oil in a large saucepan over medium-high heat and cook 1 lb cubed, boneless lean lamb for 2–3 minutes, until browned. Using a slotted spoon, transfer to a plate and set aside. Return the pan to the heat and cook the onion, garlic, ginger, cumin seeds, and chile from the main recipe for 3–4 minutes, until lightly brown. Add 2 tablespoons Madras curry paste plus 3 diced, red-skinned potatoes, cook for 1 minute, then add 1 (14½ oz) can crushed plum tomatoes and 1 cup hot lamb stock. Simmer for 15–18 minutes, or until the potatoes are tender. Return the lamb to the pan with 3 cups chopped spinach for the final 2–3 minutes and cook until the leaves have wilted.

Quick Spiced Cauliflower Pilaf

Serves 4

3 tablespoons raisins
3 cups small cauliflower florets
2 tablespoons vegetable oil
2 garlic cloves, crushed
2 scallions, thinly sliced
1½ tablespoons medium-hot
 curry paste
4 cups cooked steamed pilaf rice
chopped cilantro leaves,
 to garnish
flatbreads, to serve (optional)

- Put the raisins into a heatproof bowl, pour in 2 tablespoons boiling water, and set aside to soak.

- Cook the cauliflower florets in a large saucepan of boiling water for 4–5 minutes, until just tender.

- Meanwhile, heat the oil in a large saucepan and sauté the garlic and scallions over medium heat for 1 minute to soften. Add the curry paste and stir for 1 minute to cook the spices. Add the steamed rice and the raisins and their water, then cover and cook over medium-low heat for 2–3 minutes.

- Drain the cauliflower and fold it into the rice. Spoon into dishes, garnish with the cilantro, and serve accompanied by flatbreads, if desired.

20 Spiced Cauliflower and Cheese

Cook 7 cups large cauliflower florets in a large saucepan of boiling salted water for 8–10 minutes, or until just tender. Drain and put into 1 large or 4 individual ramekins. Meanwhile, melt 4 tablespoons butter in a large saucepan and add 1 large, finely chopped onion, 2 chopped garlic cloves, and 1 teaspoon cumin seeds. Sauté over medium heat for 6–7 minutes, stirring occasionally, until softened. Add 1 teaspoon ground coriander, ½ teaspoon turmeric, and ¼ teaspoon cayenne pepper and stir for 1 minute. Mix in 1¼ cups crème fraîche or heavy cream and 1¾ cups shredded mild cheese, such as cheddar or Monterey Jack, and stir until melted. Season to taste, then pour the sauce over the cauliflower, top with another ¾ cup grated cheese, and put under a preheated medium-hot broiler for 5–6 minutes, until bubbling and golden.

30 Aromatic Spiced Cauliflower Stew

Heat 2 tablespoons oil in a saucepan and cook 1 chopped onion, 2 chopped garlic cloves, and 1 teaspoon cumin seeds over medium heat for 6–7 minutes, stirring occasionally, until softened. Add 2 tablespoons medium-hot curry paste and stir for 1 minute. Add 5 cups cauliflower florets and 1 (15 oz) can rinsed and drained chickpeas and stir. Pour in 1 (14½ oz) can cherry or plum tomatoes plus 1 cup water, then season, cover loosely, and simmer for 15–18 minutes, until tender. Serve sprinkled with chopped cilantro and a large spoon of plain yogurt.

20 Tuna and Bulgur Wheat Bowl

Serves 4

3 cups vegetable stock
2 cups bulgur wheat
3 tablespoons olive oil
4 tuna steaks
1 (15 oz) can kidney beans,
  drained
1 cup drained canned or defrosted
  frozen corn kernels
2 scallions, finely sliced
2 roasted red peppers, drained
  and diced
small bunch of cilantro, chopped
2 tablespoons lemon juice
salt and black pepper

- Pour the stock into a saucepan, bring to a boil, and add the bulgur. Cook, uncovered, over medium heat, for 7 minutes. Cover with a tight-fitting lid and set aside for 6–7 minutes, until the liquid has been absorbed and the grains are tender.

- Meanwhile, heat a ridged grill pan over medium-high heat. Rub 1 tablespoon of the oil over the tuna steaks and season with salt and black pepper. Cook them in the grill pan for 2–3 minutes on each side, until nicely charred and cooked to your preference. Set aside and keep warm.

- Gently stir the remaining ingredients into the bulgur, then replace the lid for 3–4 minutes. Spoon the warm mixture into bowls and serve topped with the grilled tuna.

10 Quick Tuna Tabbouleh

Put 2½ cups cooked quinoa into a large bowl. Add 3 finely chopped scallions, 1 finely chopped red bell pepper, 2 tablespoons chopped parsley, 2 tablespoons chopped mint, and 8 halved cherry tomatoes. Drain and flake 2 (5 oz) cans tuna in olive oil and add to the bowl. Now add 2 tablespoons lemon juice, 2 tablespoons olive oil, and a generous pinch of salt and black pepper. Stir gently to combine and serve immediately with toasted pita breads.

30 Roasted Pumpkin with Tuna and

Bulgur Wheat Put 4 cups peeled and seeded pumpkin or butternut squash cut into ¾ inch dice into a large roasting pan. Add 2 tablespoons olive oil, 2 unpeeled garlic cloves, and 1 sliced red onion and toss together. Season generously and roast in a preheated oven, at 425°F, for 18–20 minutes, until tender. Meanwhile, cook the bulgur wheat and grill the tuna following the main recipe. Toss the cooked bulgur with the pumpkin, pile into dishes, and serve topped with the seared tuna steak and wedges of lemon, if desired.

WIN-WINT-QIL

30 Pork, Red Pepper, and Three-Bean Goulash

Serves 4

2 tablespoons olive oil

12 oz pork tenderloin, cut into thick strips

1 onion, sliced

1 red bell pepper, diced

2 garlic cloves, chopped

1 tablespoon all-purpose flour

1 tablespoon smoked paprika

2 cups mixed canned beans, such as cannellini, kidney beans, and chickpeas, rinsed and drained

1 (14½ oz) can cherry tomatoes or diced tomatoes

1 tablespoon tomato paste

1 cup hot vegetable stock

salt and black pepper

steamed greens, to serve

- Heat half the oil in a large saucepan over medium-high heat and cook the pork strips for 3–4 minutes, until browned all over. Using a slotted spoon, transfer to a plate and set aside.

- Return the pan to a medium heat with the remaining oil, then add the onion, red bell pepper, and garlic. Cook for 5–6 minutes, until softened and lightly browned.

- Reduce the heat slightly, add the flour and paprika, and stir for 1 minute. Add the beans, tomatoes, tomato paste, and stock, then season and simmer for 15–18 minutes, until rich and thick. Return the pork and its juices to the pan for the final 3–4 minutes, until heated through.

- Serve with steamed greens.

---

10 Red Pepper and Bacon Bagel

Halve 4 bagels and toast the cut sides. Meanwhile, broil 12 smoked, bacon slices under a preheated medium-hot broiler for 4–5 minutes, turning once. Put 1 teaspoon smoked paprika in a bowl and mix in 1 tablespoon chopped chives and 2 tablespoons mayonnaise. Spread over the bottom half of each bagel. Top with a small handful of baby spinach leaves and 1 drained and sliced roasted red pepper. Arrange the bacon over the roasted pepper and top with the remaining bagel halves.

20 Red Pepper, Pancetta, and Bean

Frittata Heat 2 tablespoons olive oil in a large, ovenproof skillet and cook 5 oz cubed pancetta over medium-high heat for 2–3 minutes, until golden. Add 3 drained and sliced roasted red peppers, 2 cups rinsed and drained mixed canned beans, such as kidney beans, cannellini beans, and chickpeans, and ½ cup drained and chopped sun-dried tomatoes. Stir for 2–3 minutes, until hot, then reduce the heat to medium-low. Add 4 extra-large beaten eggs with a pinch of salt and black pepper and 1 tablespoon chopped chives and stir to combine. Cook gently, without stirring, for 4–5 minutes, until the egg is almost set, then sprinkle with 1¼ cups shredded sharp cheddar cheese. Put under a preheated medium-hot broiler for 3–4 minutes, until puffed up and golden. Serve in wedges on a bed of steamed greens.

Jumbo Shrimp Soba Noodles with Sweet-and-Sour Dressing

Serves 2

10 oz raw peeled jumbo shrimp
6 oz soba noodles
½ cucumber, seeded and
   finely shredded
1–2 scallions, thinly shredded
small bunch of cilantro leaves
blanched peanuts, to sprinkle

For the dressing

2 tablespoons lime juice
1 teaspoon Thai fish sauce
1 tablespoon superfine or
   granulated sugar
2 tablespoons sweet chili sauce

- Arrange the shrimp in a steamer over a saucepan of gently simmering water and steam for 3–5 minutes, until pink and cooked. Rinse under cold water to cool and set aside.

- Bring a large saucepan of water to a boil and cook the noodles for 5–7 minutes, or according to the package directions, until tender. Drain and rinse immediately under cold water.

- Meanwhile, combine the dressing ingredients and stir until the sugar has dissolved.

- Toss the noodles in half the dressing, then combine with the cooked shrimp, cucumber, scallions, and cilantro.

- Pile into dishes and sprinkle with the peanuts. Serve drizzled with extra dressing, as desired.

Brown Egg-Fried Rice with Sweet-and-Sour Shrimp

Put 1 tablespoon oil into a wok over medium heat and stir-fry 1 sliced garlic clove, 2 teaspoons peeled and chopped fresh ginger root, and 1 sliced red chile for 2 minutes. Beat 1 egg with 2 teaspoons soy sauce and add to the pan, stirring occasionally, for 1–2 minutes. Add ⅓ cup peas, ⅓ cup corn kernels, and 2 cups steamed brown rice. Stir-fry for 3–4 minutes. Meanwhile, warm ¾ cup sweet-and-sour sauce in a saucepan with 12 oz cooked peeled shrimp for 2–3 minutes. Divide the rice between 2 dishes and spoon the shrimp and sauce over the rice.

Jumbo Shrimp and Brown Rice Stir-Fry with Sweet-and-Sour Sauce

Cook ½ cup rinsed brown rice in a large saucepan of salted boiling water for 20–25 minutes, or according to the package directions, until tender. Add ⅓ cup defrosted peas and ⅓ cup defrosted corn kernels for the final 2 minutes, then drain well. Meanwhile, lightly beat 1 extra-large egg with 2 teaspoons soy sauce. Heat 2 tablespoons oil in a large wok and stir-fry 1 sliced garlic clove, 2 teaspoons peeled and chopped fresh ginger root, and 1 seeded and sliced red chile (optional) for 1–2 minutes over medium heat, until lightly browned. Add 8 oz peeled jumbo shrimp and stir-fry for 2–3 minutes, until pink. Pour the egg into the pan and stir-fry for 1–2 minutes, until set. Transfer the rice and vegetables into the wok, stir-fry for another 2–3 minutes, until hot, then spoon into dishes. Serve immediately, drizzled with about ¾ cup warmed sweet-and-sour or sweet chili sauce.

30 Red Cabbage and Beet Stew

Serves 4–6

2 tablespoons olive oil
1 red onion, sliced
2 garlic cloves, finely chopped
1 small red cabbage, shredded
10 raw beets, peeled and cut
  into ½ inch dice
1 small cinnamon stick
generous pinch of saffron
1 teaspoon cumin seeds
1¾ cups hot lamb, chicken, or
  vegetable stock
½ cup green olives
½ small preserved lemon, chopped
salt and black pepper
chopped cilantro or parsley,
  to garnish
steamed couscous or bulgur
  wheat, to serve

- Heat the oil in a large saucepan or Dutch oven and sauté the onion and garlic over medium heat for 6–7 minutes, until softened slightly. Add the red cabbage, beets, spices, and seasoning and stir for another 1–2 minutes, until aromatic.

- Pour in the stock, season lightly, cover, and simmer gently over medium-low heat for 15–20 minutes, until the vegetables are tender. Stir in the olives and lemon for the final 10 minutes.

- Garnish the stew with the chopped herbs and serve with the couscous or bulgur.

10 Stew-Spiced Red Cabbage and Beet Salad

Shred ½ small head red cabbage. Put into a bowl with 6 raw, peeled, and coarsely grated beets and 1 peeled and coarsely grated sweet, crisp apple. In a separate bowl, combine 2 teaspoons lemon juice with 3 tablespoons olive oil, 1 teaspoon toasted cumin seeds, a pinch of ground cinnamon, and a pinch of salt and black pepper. Toss the dressing with the salad ingredients and serve sprinkled with 2 tablespoons chopped parsley or cilantro.

20 Spiced Braised Red Cabbage and Beets

Heat 2 tablespoons oil in a large saucepan and sauté 1 finely sliced red onion and 2 chopped garlic cloves for 5–6 minutes, until softened. Add 1 teaspoon cumin seeds, 1 teaspoon sweet paprika, and ½ teaspoon ground ginger and cook for 1 minute. Stir in 1 small head finely shredded red cabbage, 8 peeled and coarsely grated raw beets, 1 peeled and coarsely grated sweet, crisp apple, and ⅓ cup chopped, pitted dates (optional). Stir until hot, then pour in 1¾ cups hot chicken stock or vegetable stock with 2 teaspoons lemon juice. Simmer for 10–12 minutes, stirring occasionally, until the vegetables have softened slightly. Season to taste and serve as a side dish or accompanied by steamed couscous or bulgur wheat.

Stir-Fried Lemon Chicken with Toasted Cashew Nuts

Serves 2

1 tablespoon peanut oil
8 oz boneless, skinless chicken
    breasts, sliced
2 cups broccoli florets
1 small red bell pepper,
    coarsely chopped
2 scallions, thickly sliced
½ cup unsalted cashew nuts
1 tablespoon cornstarch
½ cup cold water
2 tablespoons lemon juice
1½ tablespoons honey
2 tablespoons light soy sauce
steamed rice or noodles, to serve
    (optional)

- Heat the oil in a large wok or skillet and cook the chicken for 3–4 minutes over medium-high heat, until golden. Using a slotted spoon, transfer to a plate and set aside.

- Return the pan to the heat and add the broccoli, red bell pepper, and scallions. Stir-fry for 3–4 minutes, until softened.

- Meanwhile, place a small saucepan over medium-low heat and toast the cashew nuts for 3–4 minutes, shaking the pan occasionally, until golden. Remove from the heat.

- Dissolve the cornstarch in a small bowl with 1 tablespoon of the water, then mix in the remaining water plus the lemon juice, honey, and soy sauce. Add to the vegetables along with the cashew nuts. Reduce the heat to medium-low and return the chicken to the pan. Simmer for 2–3 minutes, until the chicken is cooked through and the sauce is hot and thickened. Serve immediately, with steamed rice or noodles, if desired.

Crunchy Lemon Chicken Salad

Put 2 teaspoons grated lemon zest into a dish with ¾ cup dried bread crumbs. Put ⅓ cup all-purpose flour in a second dish and 1 beaten egg in a third. Dip 8 oz boneless, skinless chicken breasts sliced into large strips in the flour, then the egg followed by the bread crumbs, until coated. Heat 2 tablespoons oil in a skillet and cook the strips for 7–8 minutes, turning occasionally, until golden. Serve with salad greens, sprinkled with 2 tablespoons toasted cashew nuts and 1 sliced scallion, and a dressing of your choice.

Baked Lemony Chicken

Season 2 diced boneless, skinless chicken breasts with salt and black pepper, then place in a bowl with 2 teaspoons peanut oil and 1 teaspoon sesame oil. Add 1 coarsely chopped small red bell pepper, ½ sliced onion, and ¾ inch piece of peeled fresh ginger root cut into matchsticks. Toss everything together, then transfer into a large roasting pan and bake in a preheated oven, at 400°F, for 10 minutes, turning occasionally. Toss 2 cups broccoli florets into the pan and cook for another 5 minutes.

Meanwhile, combine the sauce ingredients from the main recipe and pour into the roasting pan with the toasted cashew nuts from the main recipe for a final 5 minutes, until the chicken is cooked and the sauce is sticky. Serve with rice or noodles.

 # Salmon and Lentil Fish Cakes

Serves 4

2 (5 oz) cans salmon, drained
2 cups cooked green lentils or
    drained, canned green lentils
2 tablespoons chopped herbs,
    such as parsley or chives
2 eggs
½ cup dried bread crumbs
2 tablespoons olive oil
salt and black pepper

To serve

green salad
tartar sauce (optional)
lemon wedges

- Put the salmon, lentils, herbs, and eggs into a food processor or bowl, add some seasoning, then pulse or stir to combine. Form into 8 fish cakes and coat in the bread crumbs. Arrange on a plate and chill for 12–15 minutes, until firm.

- Heat the oil in a large skillet over medium heat and cook the fish cakes for about 4–5 minutes, turning once, until crisp and golden. Drain on paper towels and serve with green salad and tartar sauce, if desired, and lemon wedges for squeezing over the fish.

1 Warm Salmon and Green Lentil Salad

Heat 2 tablespoons olive oil in a skillet and cook 2 chopped garlic cloves and 3 sliced scallions for 2–3 minutes, until softened. Add ½ cup chopped sun-dried tomatoes to the pan with 2 tablespoons chopped parsley and 2 cups cooked green lentils. Stir over the heat for 3–4 minutes, then add 6 oz flaked roasted salmon fillets and 1 tablespoon lemon juice. Stir gently to warm through, then spoon into 4 dishes and top each serving with a small handful of arugula leaves and 2 slices of feta, if desired.

2 Herb-Crusted Salmon with

Lentils Put 1 cup freshly made bread crumbs in a bowl with 2 tablespoons chopped parsley, 1 teaspoon grated lemon zest, 1 tablespoon finely chopped sun-dried tomatoes, and 2 finely chopped scallions. Add 1 tablespoon olive oil and mix well to combine. Put 4 boneless salmon fillets into a shallow ovenproof dish and cover with the herb topping. Place in a preheated oven, at 400°F, for 12–15 minutes, until cooked and golden. Serve immediately with 2 cups reheated cooked green lentils and an arugula and feta salad.

20 Cold-Busting Mexican Hamburgers

Serves 4

1 lb ground beef
½ small red onion, finely chopped
1 green chile, seeded and chopped
2 tablespoons mixed chopped herbs
1 egg, lightly beaten
2 teaspoons Mexican spice blend
1 teaspoon Tabasco sauce
1 cup fresh bread crumbs
salt and black pepper
2 tablespoons sunflower oil

To serve

whole-wheat burger buns
selection of toppings, such as
  salsa, avocado, and lettuce

- Combine all the burger ingredients in a large bowl and mix well. Form into 4 large patties about ¾ inch thick.

- Heat the oil in a large skillet and cook the burgers over medium heat for 8–12 minutes, turning once, until cooked to your preference.

- Serve in the burger buns with a choice of toppings, such as salsa, avocado, and lettuce.

10 Cold-Busting Beef Tostadas

Rub 2 teaspoons olive oil and 2 teaspoons Mexican-style spice blend over 2 sirloin steaks. Heat 1 tablespoon oil in a skillet and cook the steaks over medium-high heat for 4–7 minutes. Set aside. Meanwhile, toast 4 tortillas under a preheated medium-hot broiler for 2–3 minutes. Place on plates and spread 2 tablespoons salsa over each. Sprinkle with 1 cup shredded cheddar, ½ sliced red onion, ½ head shredded iceberg, and 1 diced avocado. Slice the beef, arrange over the lettuce, and serve topped with chopped cilantro, Tabasco sauce, and a squeeze of lime juice.

30 Cold-Busting Chocolate Beef

Chili Heat 2 tablespoons vegetable oil in a large saucepan and cook 1 chopped onion, 1 chopped red bell pepper, and 2 chopped garlic cloves over medium-high heat for 4–5 minutes, until slightly softened. Add 1 lb ground beef and cook for 3–4 minutes, until browned. Stir in 1 (1½ oz) package or ⅓ cup chili con carne spice mix, 1 (14½ oz) can diced tomatoes, 1 (15 oz) can drained kidney beans, ½ red wine, and ½ cup water. Bring to a boil, then reduce the heat and stir in 1 oz semisweet chocolate until melted. Cover loosely and simmer for 15–18 minutes, until rich and thick. Sprinkle with 2 tablespoons chopped cilantro and serve with warm tortillas, Tabasco sauce, and lime wedges.

20 Spiced Cabbage and Bacon Pan-Fry

Serves 2

2 tablespoons olive oil
4 oz thick bacon slices, cut into
  ½ inch strips
1 small onion, finely sliced
2 garlic cloves, chopped
pinch of ground allspice
pinch of ground cinnamon
¼ teaspoon grated nutmeg
½ small head savoy cabbage,
  thinly shredded
3 cups cauliflower florets
salt and black pepper
2 tablespoons chopped parsley,
  to garnish

- Heat the oil in a large skillet and cook the bacon for 2–3 minutes over medium-high heat, until golden. Add the onion and garlic and sauté for another 3–4 minutes, until beginning to soften.

- Stir in the spices until aromatic, then add the cabbage and cauliflower and cook, stirring, for 7–8 minutes, until slightly softened but still with some bite. Season to taste, garnish with parsley, then pile into deep bowls to serve.

10 Spiced Cabbage Coleslaw with Crispy Bacon

Core ½ small head green cabbage and slice thinly. Put into a large bowl with 1 shredded carrot, 1 finely sliced celery stick, 2 cups finely sliced cauliflower florets, and 2 thinly sliced scallions. In a separate small bowl, combine ⅔ cup sour cream, 2 teaspoons lemon juice, a pinch each of ground allspice, cinnamon, and nutmeg, 2 tablespoons chopped parsley, and salt and black pepper to taste. Pour the dressing over the vegetables and mix well. Break up 2 oz cooked smoked bacon strips over the coleslaw and serve with toasted pita breads or baked potatoes, if desired.

30 Spiced Red Cabbage with Gammon

Melt 4 tablespoons butter into a large saucepan and gently cook 1 sliced onion and 1 chopped garlic clove over medium-low heat for 5–6 minutes, until softened. Stir in the spices from the main recipe with ½ small head shredded red cabbage and 1 peeled, cored, and grated sweet, crisp apple. Cook gently for about 15 minutes, stirring frequently, until slightly softened. Meanwhile, rub 4 thick ham steaks with a little oil and arrange on an aluminum foil-lined broiler rack. Put under a preheated medium-hot broiler for 12–15 minutes, turning once, until cooked and golden but still juicy. Keep warm and set aside to rest for 2–3 minutes before serving with the spiced red cabbage.

3⓪ Cremini Mushroom and Spinach Pilaf

Serves 4

2 tablespoons vegetable oil
1 onion, finely chopped
2 garlic cloves, finely chopped
3 cups diced cremini mushrooms
3 cardamom pods, lightly crushed
¼ teaspoon ground cloves
½ teaspoon ground cinnamon
¾ cup basmati rice or other
    long-grain rice
2 cups hot vegetable stock
1 cup frozen peas, defrosted
3 cups coarsely chopped spinach
salt and black pepper
fried onions, to garnish (optional)

- Heat the oil in a large, deep skillet and cook the onion and garlic for 4–5 minutes over medium-high heat, stirring occasionally, until beginning to brown.

- Add the mushrooms, cook for 2 minutes, then add the spices and rice and stir for 1 minute.

- Pour in the stock, season generously, and cover with a tight-fitting lid. Simmer gently for about 15 minutes, until the rice grains are almost tender.

- Remove from the heat and fold in the peas and spinach. Replace the lid and set aside for 4–5 minutes, until the liquid has been absorbed and the rice is tender and light.

- Serve garnished with fried onions, if desired.

1⓪ Mushrooms and Spinach with Brown Rice Heat 2 tablespoons vegetable oil in a large skillet and sauté the onion, garlic, and mushrooms following the main recipe. Meanwhile, heat 2 (6½ oz) packages precooked brown rice or other rice according to the package directions. Stir the spices from the main recipe into the onions, then add 2 cups coarsely chopped spinach and cook, stirring, for 1–2 minutes, until wilted. Fold through the rice and serve with a dollop of Greek yogurt, and garnished with fried onions, if desired.

 2⓪ Warm Mushroom and Spinach Pâté Melt 6 tablespoons butter in a large skillet and cook 2 chopped garlic cloves and 1 lb cremini mushrooms, diced, over medium-low heat for 5–6 minutes, until tender. Stir in 3 cups chopped spinach and set aside to cool for 10 minutes. Put ⅔ cup cream cheese into a food processor with a pinch each of ground cloves and ground cinnamon and 2 tablespoons chopped parsley. Season with salt and black pepper, then add the mushrooms and spinach and pulse briefly to create a slightly warm, chunky-textured pâté. If you don't have a processor, put the cooked mushroom and spinach mixture into a bowl, beat in the cream cheese, spices, and parsley, and season with salt and black pepper. Spoon into ramekins and serve with warmed naans or chapattis.

Quick Fish Stew with Chickpeas

Serves 4

2 tablespoons olive oil
1 celery stick, thinly sliced
2 garlic cloves, chopped
1 teaspoon sweet paprika
½ cup dry white wine
2 cups prepared ratatouille
1 (15 oz) chickpeas
1 teaspoon grated lemon zest
⅓ cup vegetable stock
12 oz boneless fish fillets, such
 as halibut, cod, or salmon,
 cut into bite-size pieces
salt and black pepper
chopped parsley, to garnish
steamed whole-grain rice or
 couscous, to serve

- Heat the oil in a large saucepan and cook the celery and garlic over medium heat for 3–4 minutes, until softened.

- Add the paprika, stir for 1 minute, then pour in the wine and simmer to reduce by half.

- Add the ratatouille along with the chickpeas, lemon zest, and stock, then season to taste and simmer for 5–6 minutes, until slightly thickened.

- Stir the fish into the stew, cover, and simmer for another 3–5 minutes, or until the fish is cooked and flaky. Garnish with chopped parsley and serve with rice or couscous.

10 Pan-Fried Fish with Chickpea Ratatouille Heat 2 tablespoons oil in a large skillet and cook 4 boneless, skinless fish fillets, such as cod, halibut, red snapper, or salmon, for 5–7 minutes, turning once, until the fish is cooked and flaky. Meanwhile, in a separate saucepan, heat 2 cups prepared ratatouille with 1 (15 oz) can rinsed and drained chickpeas, 1 teaspoon finely grated lemon zest, and ½ cup hot vegetable stock. Season to taste and simmer for 4–5 minutes to let the flavors develop. Spoon into shallow dishes and serve immediately, topped with the fish and garnished with parsley.

30 One-Dish Baked Fish with Chickpeas Prepare the stew following the main recipe, adding 1 small diced head of fennel to the celery and garlic and cooking for 5–6 minutes before adding the paprika. Once the stew has simmered for 5–6 minutes, transfer to an ovenproof dish and place 4 skinless, boneless fish fillets on top. Drizzle with 1 tablespoon olive oil, season, and bake, uncovered, in a preheated oven, at 400°F, for 12–15 minutes. Serve with rice or couscous and garnished with chopped parsley.

20 Sausages with Mash Potatoes and Brussels Sprouts

Serves 2

4 Italian-style link sausages

3 Yukon gold or russet potatoes, cut into chunks

4 tablespoons butter

10 Brussels sprouts, sliced or shredded

¼ teaspoon freshly grated nutmeg

1 tablespoon chopped chives

1 tablespoon whole-grain mustard

2 tablespoons crème fraîche or heavy cream

salt and black pepper

- Arrange the sausages on an aluminum foil-lined broiler rack and put under a preheated, medium-hot broiler for 15–18 minutes, or prepare according to the package directions, until cooked through.

- Cook the potatoes in a saucepan of salted boiling water for 12–15 minutes, until tender.

- Meanwhile, melt half the butter in a skillet and cook the Brussels sprouts with the nutmeg and a generous pinch of salt and black pepper over medium-low heat for 4–6 minutes, stirring occasionally, until softened.

- Drain the potatoes, return to the pan, and mash until smooth with the remaining butter. Stir in the chives, mustard, crème fraîche, and sprouts and serve with the sausages.

10 Quick Sausage and Brussels Sprout

Pan-Fry Blanch 12 halved Brussels sprouts in a large saucepan of salted boiling water for 2–3 minutes, until just beginning to soften, then drain well. Meanwhile, heat 2 tablespoons olive oil in a large skillet and sauté 2 chopped garlic cloves over medium-low heat for 1–2 minutes, until softened. Add 8 oz sausages, cooked and sliced, and the drained Brussels sprouts, then cook, stirring, over medium-high heat for another 3–4 minutes, until just tender and golden. Serve with reheated mashed potatoes.

30 One-Pan Roasted Sausages with Brussels Sprouts

Arrange 12 oz thickly sliced herb sausages in a large roasting pan with 12 Brussels sprouts, 2 unpeeled garlic cloves, 1 small red onion cut into wedges, and 2 thyme sprigs. Season, drizzle with 2 tablespoons olive oil, and mix to coat. Roast in a preheated oven, at 425°F, for 20–25 minutes, turning occasionally, until cooked and golden. Meanwhile, prepare the mustardy mashed potatoes from the main recipe, omitting the sprouts. Serve the sausages with the mashed potatoes.

WIN-WINT-BUY

20 Spicy Sardine Linguine

Serves 4

2 tablespoons olive oil

1 red onion, chopped

2 garlic cloves, crushed

1 (14½ oz) can cherry tomatoes

½ teaspoon dried red pepper flakes

pinch of sugar

½ teaspoon finely grated lemon zest

12 oz linguine

2 (3¾ oz) cans sardines in oil, drained

2 teaspoons rinsed capers

salt and black pepper

basil leaves, to garnish (optional)

- Heat the olive oil in a large saucepan and cook the onion and garlic over medium heat for 6–7 minutes, until softened. Add the tomatoes, red pepper flakes, sugar, lemon zest, and seasoning and bring to a boil. Cover and simmer for about 10 minutes, until thickened.

- Meanwhile, cook the linguine in a large saucepan of boiling salted water for 11 minutes, or according to the package directions, until "al dente." Drain, reserving 2 tablespoons of the cooking water, and return to the pan.

- Stir the sardines and capers into the tomato sauce for the final 1–2 minutes. When hot, add to the drained pasta along with the reserved cooking water and toss gently. Serve piled into bowls and garnished with extra black pepper, and with basil leaves, if desired.

10 Quick Spicy Sardine Spaghetti

Cook 1½ lb fresh spaghetti in a large saucepan of boiling salted water for 3–4 minutes, or according to the package directions, until "al dente." Drain, reserving 3 tablespoons of the cooking water. Meanwhile, heat 2 tablespoons olive oil in a saucepan and sauté 2 chopped garlic cloves and 1 chopped red chile (seeded if less heat desired) over medium-low heat for 1–2 minutes, until softened but not browned. Add 2 (3¾ oz) cans drained, flaked sardines in oil, 1 tablespoon lemon juice, and 2 teaspoons rinsed capers. Warm through for 2–3 minutes, then pour over the spaghetti, add the reserved cooking water and 2 tablespoons chopped parsley or basil, and toss together. Season to taste and serve.

30 Spicy Tomato and Sardine Pasta

Casserole Make the tomato sauce with sardines following the main recipe, but reduce the simmering time to 5 minutes so that the sauce is less thick. Meanwhile, cook 12 oz penne pasta in a large saucepan of boiling salted water until "al dente." Stir into the sauce, transfer into a large, ovenproof dish, and top with 4 oz halved mini mozzarella balls. Bake in a preheated oven, at 400°F, for 15–18 minutes, or until golden and bubbling.

QuickCook

Comfort-Food Main Dishes

Recipes listed by cooking time

30

2

 # Creamy Butternut and Sage Orzo

Serves 4

4 tablespoons butter

2–3 banana shallots, chopped

2 garlic cloves, chopped

2 cups finely chopped, peeled, and seeded butternut squash

8 oz orzo pasta

3 tablespoons pine nuts

3 cups hot vegetable stock

½ tablespoon chopped sage

½ cup mascarpone

¼ cup freshly grated Parmesan cheese

salt and black pepper

To garnish

shredded sage leaves

Parmesan shavings (optional)

- Melt the butter in a large, deep skillet and sauté the shallots, garlic, and squash over medium heat for 6–7 minutes. Stir in the orzo until coated.

- Meanwhile, toast the pine nuts in a small, dry skillet over medium-low heat for 3–4 minutes, shaking the pan often, until golden. Transfer onto a small plate and set aside.

- Pour the stock into the orzo, and add the sage and a pinch of salt and black pepper. Bring to a boil, then cover with a lid and simmer for about 10 minutes, stirring occasionally to prevent the pasta from sticking, until the liquid has been absorbed and the squash and pasta are tender.

- Stir the mascarpone and grated Parmesan into the orzo and set aside to rest for 1–2 minutes.

- Spoon the mixture into bowls and sprinkle with the toasted pine nuts, the shredded sage leaves, and a few Parmesan shavings, if desired.

 Quick Sage Risotto with Pine Nuts

Melt 4 tablespoons butter in a skillet and cook 3 chopped shallots and 2 chopped garlic cloves for 3–4 minutes, until softened. Toast the pine nuts as in the main recipe. Stir 4 cups cooked whole-grain rice into the pan with ⅓ cup hot vegetable stock, ½ cup mascarpone, 1 tablespoon chopped sage, and 3 tablespoons grated Parmesan cheese. Season to taste and simmer for for 2–3 minutes, until hot and creamy. Serve as above.

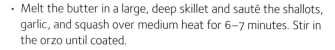 **Rainy-Day Butternut and Sage Risotto** Melt 4 tablespoons butter in a large skillet and sauté 3 finely chopped banana shallots, 2 chopped garlic cloves, and 2 cups peeled, seeded, and finely diced butternut squash for 6–7 minutes, until softened. Add 1 tablespoon chopped sage with 2 cups risotto rice and stir until the grains are coated and looking translucent. Pour in ½ cup dry white wine and simmer rapidly, stirring until completely evaporated. Add 5 cups boiling vegetable stock, a ladleful at a time, stirring constantly at a gentle simmer until each ladleful has been absorbed and the rice is "al dente." This process should take about 17 minutes. Stir 2 tablespoons mascarpone into the risotto, then cover and set aside to rest for 1–2 minutes before serving as above.

WIN-COMF-CYA

Pan-Fried Polenta Fries with Arrabbiata Sauce

Serves 2

1 (1 lb) log store-bought polenta

3 tablespoons all-purpose flour, for dusting

¼ cup olive oil

1½ cups store-bought arrabbiata pasta sauce

arugula and Parmesan salad, to serve

- Cut the log of polenta into fry-shaped strips and dust in the flour, shaking off the excess.

- Heat the oil in a skillet and cook the polenta fries over medium-high heat for 2–3 minutes on each side, until crisp and golden. Drain on paper towels and keep warm.

- Meanwhile, heat the arrabbiata sauce in a saucepan. Spoon into small bowls and serve with the polenta fries and salad.

Soft Polenta Arrabbiata

Heat 2 tablespoons olive oil in a large saucepan over medium heat and cook 1 small chopped red onion, 1 chopped garlic clove, and 1 chopped red chile for 6–7 minutes, until softened. Add 2 ripe diced tomatoes, ½ cup sliced pitted green olives, and 2 tablespoons chopped parsley. Season with salt and black pepper and stir occasionally for 3–4 minutes, until the tomatoes begin to collapse. Meanwhile, cook 1 cup instant polenta or cornmeal according to the package directions, until soft. Stir in 2 tablespoons grated Parmesan cheese, 1 tablespoon chopped parsley, and a generous pinch of salt and black pepper, then spoon the polenta into dishes. Serve with the warm arrabbiata sauce, an arugula salad, and extra Parmesan, if desired.

Baked Polenta with Arrabbiata

Sauce Pour 1½ cups store-bought arrabbiata sauce into the bottom of a medium ovenproof dish. Lay 10 oz sliced polenta over the sauce and top with ½ cup diced mozzarella and 2 tablespoons grated Parmesan. Pour the remaining sauce over the top and sprinkle with ¾ cup diced mozzarella and 2 tablespoons grated Parmesan. Bake in a preheated oven, at 425°F, for 20–25 minutes, until golden and bubbling. Serve with a salad, as above.

30 Rich and Comforting Baked Beans with Sausages

Serves 4

2 tablespoons olive oil

8 oz pancetta or bacon, chopped

2 banana shallots, finely chopped

2 garlic cloves, chopped

1 celery stick, thinly sliced

1 carrot, diced

1 teaspoon sweet paprika

½ cup red wine

2 (15 oz) cans navy beans
   or cannellini beans, rinsed
   and drained

2 cups tomato puree or
   tomato sauce

1 teaspoon red wine vinegar

1 tablespoon Worcestershire sauce

1 tablespoon packed dark
   brown sugar

salt and black pepper

8 herby sausages, grilled, to serve

- Heat the oil in a large saucepan and cook the pancetta or bacon over medium-high heat for 3–4 minutes, until golden. Add the shallots, garlic, celery, and carrot. Cook for 7–8 minutes, until softened, adding the paprika for the final minute.

- Pour in the wine and simmer until completely evaporated, Add the beans, tomato puree or tomato sauce, vinegar, Worcestershire sauce, and sugar. Season to taste and simmer for about 15 minutes, stirring occasionally, until rich and thick, adding a little water, if necessary.

- Slice the sausages thickly and serve with the beans.

10 Smoky Sausage and Beans on Garlic

Toast Heat 2 tablespoons olive oil in a large skillet and sauté 1 finely chopped onion and 1 thinly sliced celery stick for 6–7 minutes, to soften. Add 8 oz thickly sliced smoked link sausages and 1 teaspoon sweet smoked paprika and cook for 1 minute. Add 1 (15 oz) can navy beans plus 2 cups store-bought tomato and basil pasta sauce. Bring to a boil and serve spooned over toasted garlic bread slices.

20 Quick Baked Eggs and Beans

Prepare the beans following the 10-minute recipe, but omitting the sausage. Divide the mixture among 4 individual ovenproof dishes, then crack an egg into the center of each one. Bake in a preheated oven, 400°F, for 8–10 minutes, until the egg white is set but the yolk still soft. Serve with cooked sausages and crusty garlic bread, if desired.

20 Chicken and Brie Puff Pie

Serves 4

1 sheet ready-to-bake
   puff pastry
1 medium egg, beaten
1 tablespoon olive oil
2 leeks, chopped
2 cups halved baby button
   mushrooms halved
2½ cups diced, cooked chicken
4 oz Brie cheese, sliced
4 slices of prosciutto, cut
   into strips
1 teaspoon chopped thyme
   leaves (optional)
¼ cup crème fraîche or
   heavy cream
salt and black pepper

- Line a baking sheet with parchment paper. Unroll the pastry, place a pie dish on it upside down, and cut around it. Place the pastry on the prepared sheet, brush with beaten egg, and bake in a preheated oven, at 400°F, for about 10 minutes, until puffed up and pale golden.

- Meanwhile, heat the oil in a large skillet and sauté the leeks for 3–4 minutes, until softened. Add the mushrooms and cook for another 3–4 minutes, until soft and golden. Add the remaining ingredients and season to taste.

- Once the chicken is hot, put the filling into the pie dish, top with the pastry lid, and return to the oven for 3–4 minutes, or until the pastry is golden and crisp.

---

10 Chicken, Brie, and Thyme Melts

Split 1 French bread in half lengthwise and then widthwise to make 4 equal pieces. Spread each cut side with 2 tablespoons onion chutney. Divide 8 oz thickly sliced chicken, 4 oz sliced Brie, 8 halved cherry tomatoes, and 1 teaspoon thyme equally among each on the bread pieces. Drizzle each slice with ½ teaspoon olive oil, place on a broiler rack, and heat under a preheated medium-hot broiler for 5–6 minutes, until melted and golden. Serve with arugula.

30 Chicken, Brie, and Leek Pies

Melt 4 tablespoons butter in a large skillet over medium heat and cook 2 sliced leeks and 2 cups sliced mushrooms for 6–7 minutes, until softened. Meanwhile, unroll 1 sheet of store-bought puff pastry and cut into 4 circles a little larger than the top of 4 individual pie dishes. Cut 4 roasted chicken breasts into bite-size pieces and add to the pan with 4 slices prosciutto cut into strips, 1 teaspoon chopped thyme, and ⅔ cup light cream. Heat to boiling point, then divide among the pie dishes. Slice 4 oz Brie and put 1 or 2 slices on top of the filling. Cover each dish with a pastry lid, letting it overhang slightly. Brush with beaten egg, cut a steam hole in the top of each pie, and bake in a preheated oven, at 400°F, for about 15 minutes, until the pastry is puffed up and golden.

 Crispy Pork Milanese with Root Vegetable Coleslaw

Serves 4

8 pork tenderloin medallions

3 tablespoons all-purpose flour, seasoned

2 medium eggs, beaten

2 cups fresh bread crumbs

2 parsnips, shredded

6 carrots, shredded

1 small sweet, crisp apple, peeled, cored, and coarsely grated

1 tablespoon chopped dill or parsley

¼ cup crème fraîche or sour cream

1 tablespoon whole-grain mustard

2 teaspoons cider vinegar

3 tablespoons olive oil

salt and black pepper

lemon wedges, to garnish

- Put the pork medallions between 2 large pieces of plastic wrap and bash with a rolling pin to flatten them to a thickness of ¼ inch.

- Put the flour, eggs, and bread crumbs into three separate shallow dishes. Dip the pork first in the flour, then the egg, and finally the bread crumbs.

- Put the parsnips, carrots, and apple into a bowl, add the dill, crème fraîche or sour cream, mustard, vinegar, and a pinch of salt and black pepper, and mix well.

- Heat the oil in a large skillet and cook the pork over medium heat for 4–5 minutes, turning once, until cooked and golden. Spoon the coleslaw onto plates and serve with the crispy pork Milanese, garnished with lemon wedges.

Pan-Fried Pork with Root Vegetable Coleslaw Heat 2 tablespoons olive oil in a skillet and cook 4 seasoned pork cutlets for 3–4 minutes each side, or until cooked and golden. Meanwhile, prepare the coleslaw following the main recipe. Serve with the pan-fried pork.

Pork Tenderloin with Mashed Root Vegetables Cut 2 thin pork tenderloins in half. Slice 2 garlic cloves into little matchsticks. Make small slits in the pork and stuff with the garlic and the leaves from 1 rosemary sprig. Put into a small roasting pan and drizzle with 1 tablespoon olive oil. Season with salt and black pepper and place in a preheated oven, at 425°F, for 15–20 minutes, until just cooked. Meanwhile, chop 2 lb root vegetables, such as potatoes, parsnips, celeriac, and carrots, into chunks and cook in a large saucepan of lightly salted water for 12–15 minutes, until tender. Drain and return to the pan with 2 tablespoons crème fraîche or heavy cream, 1 tablespoon whole-grain mustard, 2 tablespoons chopped parsley, and a generous pinch of salt and black pepper. Mash until smooth and keep warm. Remove the pork from the oven and set aside to rest for 1–2 minutes, before serving with the mashed root vegetables.

30 Cheesy Tuna and Chive Pastries

Serves 4

4 tablespoons butter
2 leeks, finely sliced
1 (1 lb) package store-bought
   puff pastry
flour, for dusting
2 (5 oz) cans tuna in olive oil,
   drained
¾ cup cold mashed potatoes
1 cup shredded sharp
   cheddar cheese
1½ tablespoons chopped chives
1 medium egg, lightly beaten
salt and black pepper
salad greens, to serve (optional)

- Line a baking sheet with parchment paper.

- Melt the butter in a large skillet and cook the leeks for 4–5 minutes, until softened.

- Meanwhile, roll out the pastry on a lightly floured work surface and stamp out four 8½ inch circles.

- Transfer the leeks to a large bowl, add the tuna, mashed potatoes, cheese, chives, and a pinch of salt and black pepper, and mix well.

- Spoon the mixture into the middle of each pastry circle, then brush a little beaten egg around the border. Fold up the pastry, pinching and crimping the edges together encase the filling.

- Arrange the pasties on the prepared baking sheet, brush with beaten egg, and bake in a preheated oven, at 425°F, for about 15 minutes, or until puffed and golden. Cool slightly and serve with salad greens, if desired.

---

10 Grilled Tuna and Chive Sandwiches

Put the tuna, cheese, and chives from the main recipe into a bowl. Add ¼ cup mayonnaise and 1 teaspoon lemon juice, season, and mix well. Spread thickly over 4 slices of country-style bread. Place a small handful of baby spinach or arugula leaves on each, then top with another slice of bread. Toast in a dry skillet for 3–4 minutes, turning once. Alternatively, toast in a grilling machine following the manufacturer's directions, until melting and golden.

20 Quick Tuna and Chive Rissoles

Cook the leeks in the melted butter, as in the main recipe. Meanwhile, put ½ cup cooked rice, 1 cup freshly made bread crumbs, and 1 extra-large beaten egg in a bowl or food processor. Add the tuna, cheese, and chives from the main recipe, then the softened leek, and stir or pulse briefly to combine. Shape into about 12 rissoles and dust lightly in all-purpose flour, shaking off the excess. Heat 3 tablespoons olive oil in a large skillet over medium heat and cook the rissoles for 3–5 minutes, turning once, until crisp and golden. Serve with tartar sauce and salad greens, if desired.

Beef Bourguignon

Serves 2

3 tablespoons olive oil
4 oz bacon, chopped
3 oz portobello mushrooms, sliced
2 tenderloin steaks
½ cup red wine
½ cup good-quality beef stock
2 tablespoons cold butter, diced
salt and black pepper
mashed potatoes, to serve

- Heat half the olive oil in a large skillet and cook the bacon over medium-high heat for 2–3 minutes, until golden. Add the mushrooms and cook for another 2–3 minutes, until softened and golden.

- Meanwhile, heat the remaining oil in a separate skillet and cook the steaks over medium-high heat for 2–3 minutes on each side, or until cooked to your preference. Transfer to a plate and keep warm.

- Pour the wine into the empty pan and stir over medium-low heat, scraping up any sediment stuck to the bottom of the pan, until the wine becomes syrupy. Add to the bacon mixture, then pour in the stock and simmer hard to reduce by half. Season to taste, then gradually whisk in the butter until the sauce is smooth and glossy.

- Arrange the steaks on warm plates and serve immediately with the bourguignon sauce and hot mashed potatoes.

20 Quick Boeuf Bourguignon

Heat 2 tablespoons olive oil in a skillet and add 10 oz top sirloin steak cut into thick strips. Cook over high heat for 3–4 minutes, until browned. Transfer to a plate and set aside. Return the pan to a medium-high heat and cook 4 oz cubed pancetta for 2–3 minutes, until golden. Add 4 quartered small shallots, sauté for 3–4 minutes, until golden, then add 2 cups halved baby button mushrooms and sauté for 2–3 minutes. Pour in 2 tablespoons brandy and ½ cup red wine and heat until reduced and syrupy. Add ½ cup beef stock and simmer to reduce by half. Return the meat to the pan, heat through, and serve with hot mashed potatoes.

30 Burgundy-Style Beef Pies

Make the boeuf bourguignon as in the 20-minute recipe, then spoon into 2 individual pie dishes. Meanwhile, chop 4 russet potatoes into chunks and cook in a saucepan of salted boiling water for 12–15 minutes. Drain and return to the pan with 4 tablespoons butter and a pinch of nutmeg, salt, and black pepper. Mash until smooth, then spoon over the pie filling and sprinkle with ¼ cup shredded cheddar cheese. Put under a preheated medium-hot broiler for 6–7 minutes, until golden.

20 Tortellini Casserole with Cheese and Bacon

Serves 4

1 (20 oz) package fresh tortellini, such as tomato and basil

2 tablespoons olive oil

8 oz bacon, diced

2 cups sliced button mushrooms (optional)

1²⁄₃ cups crème fraîche or heavy cream

½ cup crumbled blue cheese, such as Stilton or Roquefort

black pepper

1 cup shredded cheddar cheese

green salad, to serve (optional)

- Cook the pasta in a large saucepan of lightly salted boiling water for 2–3 minutes, or according to the package directions, until tender. Drain, reserving 3 tablespoons of the cooking water, then transfer the tortellini into 1 large or 4 individual ovenproof dishes.

- Meanwhile, heat the oil in a skillet and cook the bacon over medium heat for 4–5 minutes, until browned. Add the mushrooms and cook for another 3–4 minutes, until golden.

- Stir in the crème fraîche and reserved cooking water, the blue cheese, and a pinch of black pepper. Heat gently until the cheese has melted, then pour the mixture over the pasta.

- Sprinkle with the cheddar and slide the dish(es) under a preheated medium-hot broiler for 6–7 minutes, or until bubbling and golden. Serve with a green salad, if desired.

---

10 Cheesy Penne with Crispy Bacon

Broil 8 bacon slices under a preheated medium-hot broiler for 6–7 minutes. Cook 1 ½ lb fresh penne pasta in a saucepan of salted boiling water for 2–3 minutes. Drain and return to the pan with 2 tablespoons of the cooking water. Meanwhile, melt 2 tablespoons butter in a skillet and cook 2 cups sliced mushrooms for 3–4 minutes. Stir in the crème fraîche, blue cheese, and black pepper from the main recipe. When the cheese has melted, stir the mixture into the pasta. Crumble the crispy bacon over the top and serve immediately.

30 Crunchy-Topped Macaroni and Cheese

Cook 12 oz macaroni or other pasta tubes in a large saucepan of lightly salted boiling water for 10 minutes, or according to the package directions, until "al dente." Meanwhile, cook the bacon and mushrooms following the main recipe. Put 2½ cups milk in a saucepan with ²⁄₃ cup all-purpose flour and 6 tablespoons butter and bring slowly to a boil, stirring constantly with a wire whisk, until thick and smooth. Simmer for 1–2 minutes, then season lightly. Remove from the heat and stir in ²⁄₃ cup crumbled blue cheese and season with plenty of black pepper. Mix with the drained pasta, bacon, and mushrooms, then place in a large, ovenproof dish. Top with 2 tablespoons grated Parmesan cheese and 2 tablespoons fresh bread crumbs and bake in a preheated oven, at 425°F, for about 15 minutes, until the top is golden and crunchy.

30 Roasted Chicken and Winter Vegetables

Serves 4

¼ cup olive oil
4 chicken breasts, skin on
12 oz new potatoes, halved
6 carrots, quartered
3 parsnips, cored and quartered
4 banana shallots, quartered
6 small garlic cloves
2 thyme sprigs
rosemary sprig
salt and black pepper
steamed kale, to serve (optional)

• Heat half the oil in a large skillet over medium-high heat and cook the chicken, skin side down without moving, for 7–8 minutes, until the skin is really crisp and golden.

• Meanwhile, parboil the potatoes in a large saucepan of salted boiling water for 6–7 minutes, adding the carrots and parsnips for the final 3 minutes. They should all be starting to soften.

• Drain well and put into a large roasting pan. Add the shallots, garlic, herbs, and remaining oil, season generously, and toss well. Nestle the chicken in with the vegetables, skin side up.

• Roast in a preheated oven, at 425°F, for about 20 minutes, until the chicken is cooked and the vegetables are golden. Serve with steamed kale, if desired.

---

1 Hearty Roasted Chicken Salad

Heat 2 tablespoons olive oil in a skillet and cook 8 oz chopped pancetta or smoked bacon over medium-high heat for 3–4 minutes, until golden. Transfer to a plate and keep hot. Add 12 oz sliced, cooked new potatoes and cook for 4–5 minutes, turning occasionally, until lightly golden. Meanwhile, remove the meat from 1 small roasted chicken or 4 cooked chicken legs in large pieces and arrange on serving plates with 5 cups salad greens. Sprinkle the bacon and potatoes over the top and serve immediately with your preferred dressing.

2 Pan-Fried Chicken with Roasted Vegetables

Transfer 1 (1 lb) package of mixed vegetables, such as cabbage, carrots, and broccoli, to a large roasting pan with 1 lb halved new potatoes. Toss with 3 tablespoons olive oil, 2 thyme sprigs, and a generous pinch of salt and black pepper. Roast in a preheated oven, at 450°F, for 18 minutes, shaking the pan occasionally, until tender and golden. Meanwhile, heat 2 tablespoons olive oil in a large skillet and cook 4 seasoned chicken breasts, skin side down, for 8–10 minutes, until really golden. Turn the chicken and cook for another 3–5 minutes, or until the juices run clear.

Serve the chicken with the roasted vegetables.

Comforting Fish Casserole

Serves 4

6 russet or Yukon gold potatoes, cut into chunks

2 eggs (optional)

1¾ cups milk

⅓ cup all-purpose flour

1 stick butter

2 tablespoons chopped parsley

1 cup coarsely chopped watercress (optional)

1 (14 oz) package mixed fish chunks, or boneless, skinless salmon, red snapper, cod, and/ or halibut cut into bite-size chunks

8 oz raw peeled jumbo shrimp

3 tablespoons crème fraîche or heavy cream

¾ cup shredded cheddar cheese

green salad, to serve

salt and black pepper

- Cook the potatoes in a saucepan of lightly salted boiling water for 10–12 minutes, until tender.

- Hard-boil the eggs, if using, in a saucepan of simmering water for about 8 minutes. Drain and hold under cold running water. Once cool enough to handle, remove the shells and cut the eggs into wedges.

- Put the milk, flour, and half the butter into a saucepan and bring slowly to a boil, stirring constantly with a wire whisk, until thick and smooth. Simmer for 1–2 minutes, then season lightly and remove from the heat.

- Stir the parsley, watercress (if using), fish, shrimp, and egg into the sauce, then transfer to an ovenproof dish.

- Drain the potatoes and mash them with the crème fraîche or heavy cream and the remaining butter. Season to taste, then spoon the mashed potatoes over the fish mixture and sprinkle with the shredded cheese. Place the casserole in a preheated oven, at 425°F, for 12–15 minutes, until golden and bubbling and the fish is cooked. Serve with green salad.

1 Creamy Fish with Mashed Potatoes

Heat 2 cups store-bought mashed potatoes according to the package directions. Melt 4 tablespoons butter in a skillet and cook 4 seasoned white fish fillets over medium-low heat for 5–7 minutes, turning once, until flaky. Pour in 1 cup store-bought dill sauce or other herb sauce and heat for 1–2 minutes, then serve with the mashed potatoes and a green salad.

2 Quick Fish Gratin

Pour 1 cup Alfredo sauce into a saucepan with the fish mixture and jumbo shrimp used in the main recipe. Warm gently until boiling, then simmer for 2–3 minutes, until the fish is just cooked. Transfer to an ovenproof dish. Top with 4 cooked, sliced red-skinned potatoes, dot with 4 tablespoons butter, and sprinkle with ¾ cup shredded sharp cheddar cheese. Put under a preheated medium-hot broiler for 7–8 minutes, until golden and bubbling. Serve with a watercress salad.

 # Gnocchi Gratin with Sun-Dried Tomato and Mascarpone

Serves 2

½ cup drained and chopped
    sun-dried tomatoes
⅓ cup drained roasted
    red peppers
3 tablespoons freshly grated
    Parmesan cheese
½ cup mascarpone cheese
1 tablespoon chopped basil
1 (16 oz) package gnocchi
salt and black pepper
arugula and Parmesan salad,
    to serve (optional)

- Put the tomatoes and roasted peppers into a blender or food processor and blend to a chunky paste. Transfer to a bowl and beat in 1 tablespoon of the Parmesan, the mascarpone, basil, and a pinch of salt and black pepper.

- Cook the gnocchi in a large saucepan of salted boiling water for 1–3 minutes, or according to the package directions, until they float to the surface. Drain and transfer into 1 medium or 2 individual ovenproof dishes.

- Spoon the mascarpone mixture evenly over the gnocchi, sprinkle with the remaining Parmesan, and put under a preheated medium-hot broiler for 6–8 minutes, until bubbling and golden. Cool slightly before serving with an arugula and Parmesan salad, if desired.

Sun-Dried Tomato and Gnocchi Salad Bowl Heat 1 tablespoon olive oil in a large skillet and sauté 1 (16 oz) package fresh potato gnocchi for 6–7 minutes, tossing frequently, until crisp and golden. Meanwhile, gently combine 3 cups arugula with the sun-dried tomatoes, roasted red peppers, and basil from the main recipe. Pile into 2 pasta bowls and top with the gnocchi. Sprinkle each serving with a small handful of Parmesan shavings, plus a drizzle of olive oil and balsamic glaze.

 Gnocchi Casserole with Sun-Dried Tomato and Mascarpone Heat 1 tablespoon olive oil in a skillet and sauté 2 chopped shallots and 1 chopped garlic clove over medium heat for 3–4 minutes, until beginning to soften. Stir in 1 (14½ oz) can cherry tomatoes or diced tomatoes, 1 cup chopped sun-dried tomatoes, and ½ cup roasted red peppers. Simmer for 5–6 minutes, until thickened slightly, then stir in ½ cup mascarpone. Add 1 (16 oz) package fresh gnocchi and 1 tablespoon chopped basil, bring to a boil, and season to taste. Transfer to an ovenproof dish and sprinkle 2 tablespoons freshly grated Parmesan over the top. Bake in a preheated oven, at 400°F, for about 15 minutes, until bubbling and golden. Serve as above.

Cheese and Onion on Toast

Serves 4

⅓ cup caramelized onion
  or onion chutney
4 large slices of sourdough bread,
  lightly toasted
⅔ cup store-bought cheese
  sauce or Alfredo sauce
1⅓ cups shredded sharp
  cheddar cheese
2 tablespoons whole-grain
  mustard
2 egg yolks
salt and black pepper

To serve

Worcestershire sauce (optional)
green salad

- Spread the chutney over the toasted bread.

- Put all the remaining ingredients into a bowl and beat together. Season to taste and spread over the toasts.

- Place under a preheated medium-hot broiler for 4–6 minutes, or until the topping is melting and golden. Serve with Worcestershire sauce, if desired, and a green salad.

Cheese and Onion Pizza

Mix 1 tablespoon whole-grain mustard with ⅔ cup store-bought cheese sauce or Alfredo sauce and 2 tablespoons caramelized onions. Spread thinly over 2 store-bought pizza crusts. Top with 1 small, thinly sliced red onion and ¾ cup pitted black ripe olives. Place in a preheated oven, at 400°F, for 12–15 minutes, until crisp. Serve with a salad, as above.

Cheese, Potato, and Onion

Turnovers Melt 2 tablespoons butter in a large skillet with 1 tablespoon olive oil. Cook 1 thinly sliced onion over medium heat for 6–7 minutes, until softened. Meanwhile, unroll 1 sheet of puff pastry and cut into 4 equal rectangles. Dice 1 large cooked potato and put into a bowl with 1 cup shredded sharp cheddar cheese, ½ cup crumbled Stilton or other blue cheese, 1 tablespoon whole-grain mustard, 2 tablespoons chopped parsley, and a generous pinch of black pepper. Add the softened onion and mix well. Divide the mixture among the pastry rectangles, then brush the border with a little beaten egg and fold the pastry over the filling, pinching the edges to seal. Brush the top with beaten egg, place on a baking sheet lined with parchment paper, and bake in a preheated oven, at 425°F, for 15–18 minutes, until puffed up and golden.

 Cajun-Spiced Turkey Meatballs

Serves 4

6 sweet potatoes (about 2 lb),
  cut into thin wedges
¼ cup vegetable oil
1 small red onion, sliced
1 red bell pepper, seeded
  and sliced
2 garlic cloves
4 teaspoons Cajun spice blend
3 cups tomato puree or
  tomato sauce
pinch of sugar
salt and black pepper
sour cream, to serve (optional)

For the meatballs

1 lb ground turkey
2 teaspoons Cajun spice blend
2 scallions, finely chopped
1 cup fresh bread crumbs
2 tablespoons chopped cilantro

- Place the sweet potatoes in a roasting pan with half the oil and season. Toss well, then roast in a preheated oven, at 425°F, for 20–25 minutes, until golden and tender.

- Meanwhile, combine all the meatball ingredients in a bowl, adding some salt and black pepper. Roll into 20–24 balls. Heat the remaining oil in a large saucepan and cook the meatballs over medium-high heat for 3–4 minutes, shaking the pan occasionally, until browned. Transfer to a plate and set aside.

- Return the saucepan to the heat and cook the onion, bell pepper, and garlic for 7–8 minutes, until softened and lightly browned. Add the spice mix and stir over medium heat for 1 minute. Pour in the tomato puree or sauce, add a pinch of salt, black pepper, and sugar, and simmer for 5–6 minutes, until slightly thickened.

- Add the meatballs to the sauce and simmer for 6–7 minutes, until cooked and the sauce has thickened. Serve with the sweet potato wedges and a dollop of sour cream, if desired.

1 Cajun-Spiced Turkey Burgers

Make the meatball mixture as in the main recipe, then form into 4 large patties. Heat 2 tablespoons oil in a large skillet and cook the patties over medium-high heat for 7–8 minutes, turning once, until cooked and golden. Place inside 4 warm burger buns and serve immediately with any desired toppings, such as spicy salsa, thinly sliced red onion, and red bell pepper.

2 Cajun-Spiced Turkey Fajitas

Thinly slice 1 lb turkey cutlets. Put into a bowl with 1 tablespoon Cajun spice and mix well to coat. Heat 2 tablespoons vegetable oil in a skillet and sauté 1 sliced onion and 1 seeded and sliced red bell pepper, stirring, over medium-high heat for 3–4 minutes, until lightly charred but still firm. Transfer to a plate, then return the pan to medium-high heat and cook the turkey strips, stirring, for 6–7 minutes, until cooked through. Meanwhile, warm 4 large, soft flour tortillas according to the package directions. Return the onion and red pepper to the pan and mix well. Fill the tortillas with the turkey filling, then roll up and serve immediately with spicy salsa and jalapeño peppers, if desired.

Creamy Chicken and Mushroom Rice

Serves 4

4 tablespoons butter

3 scallions, sliced

2 cooked chicken breasts, sliced or shredded

2½ cups long-grain and wild rice mixture

1½ (6 oz) jars sliced mushrooms, drained

¼ cup crème fraîche or heavy cream

salt and black pepper

- Melt the butter in a large skillet and cook the scallions for 2–3 minutes over medium heat, until softened. Add the chicken, rice, and all but a small handful of the mushrooms. Stir-fry for 3–4 minutes, until piping hot.

- Add the crème fraîche, season to taste, and stir occasionally for about 2 minutes, until hot and creamy. Spoon into shallow bowls and serve immediately, topped with the reserved mushrooms.

Chicken and Mushroom Fried Rice

Cook 2 cups instant long-grain rice for 8–9 minutes, or according to the package directions, until just tender. Drain well. Heat 2 tablespoons vegetable oil in a large skillet or wok and sauté 3 sliced scallions with 2 chopped garlic cloves for 2–3 minutes. Add 3 cups diced cremini mushrooms and the shredded chicken from the main recipe and stir-fry for 3–4 minutes, until soft and golden. Increase the heat slightly and add the rice plus ½ cup defrosted peas. Stir-fry for 3–4 minutes, until hot and lightly golden. Season to taste, then spoon into bowls and serve with soy sauce.

Chicken and Wild Mushroom Risotto

Put ½ oz dried mushrooms in a saucepan with 5 cups chicken stock, then cover and simmer for about 10 minutes. Meanwhile, melt 4 tablespoons butter in a skillet and cook 1 finely chopped onion and 2 chopped garlic cloves for 5–6 minutes, until softened. Add 3 cups diced cremini mushrooms and cook for another 2–3 minutes, until softened. Add 2 cups risotto rice and stir until the grains are coated and translucent. Pour in ½ cup dry vermouth or dry white wine and simmer rapidly, stirring constantly, until it has been absorbed. Drain the dried mushrooms, returning the stock to the pan and keeping it hot. Add the stock to the rice, a ladleful at a time, stirring constantly at a gentle simmer until each ladleful has been absorbed. Continue until all of the stock has been used and the rice is "al dente." This should take about 17 minutes. Coarsely chop the dried mushrooms and stir into the rice. Serve with grated Parmesan, if desired.

 # Deep-Pan Meat-Feast Pizza

Serves 2

1²⁄₃ cups all-purpose flour

2½ teaspoons baking powder

½ teaspoon salt

½ teaspoon ground black pepper

1 teaspoon dried oregano

2 medium eggs, lightly beaten

¼ cup tomato paste

1 tablespoon olive oil

3–4 tablespoons milk

4 oz thinly sliced meats, such as
   salami, prosciutto, pepperoni,
   and/or garlic sausage

4 oz mozzarella cheese,
   thinly sliced

½ cup mixed pitted olives
   (optional)

chili oil, to drizzle (optional)

mixed salad, to serve (optional)

- Sift the flour and baking powder into a bowl, then add the salt, black pepper, and oregano.

- Add the eggs, half the tomato paste, the olive oil, and enough milk to create a soft dough. Flatten into 1 or 2 circles about ½ inch thick and place on a baking sheet.

- Spread the remaining tomato paste over the pizza crust(s) and top them with the sliced meats, mozzarella, and olives. Bake in a preheated oven, at 400°F, for 10–15 minutes, until the crust is crisp and the topping melted. Cut into wedges, drizzle with chili oil, if desired, and serve with a mixed salad, if desired.

 ### Meat-Feast Pita Pizza

Spread 2 tablespoons tomato paste or pizza sauce over 2 large pita breads. Top with the mozzarella, sliced meats, and olives from the main recipe. Arrange on baking sheets and place in a preheated oven, at 400°F, for 5–7 minutes, until crisp and melting. Serve as above.

Skillet Meat-Feast Pizza

Mix 1¼ cups all-purpose flour in a bowl with ½ teaspoon dried oregano and a generous pinch of salt and black pepper. Pour in ⅓ cup warm water and 2 teaspoons olive oil and knead to form a smooth dough. Roll out to fit a large skillet and dust with a little flour. Heat the skillet over medium heat. When hot, add the dough and cook for about 10 minutes, turning once, until lightly golden. Spread 2 tablespoons pizza sauce over the pizza crust and sprinkle with the mozzarella, meats, and olives from the main recipe. Place under a preheated, medium-hot broiler for 3–5 minutes, until golden and bubbling, then serve as above.

Quick-Fried Steak Stroganoff

Serves 2

2 tablespoons butter

1½ tablespoons olive oil

2 shallots, finely chopped

2 cups sliced cremini mushrooms

2 teaspoons sweet paprika

⅔ cup sour cream

1 teaspoon rinsed and drained green peppercorns

2 sirloin steaks

1–2 tablespoons chopped parsley

salt and black pepper

cooked mixed long-grain and wild rice, to serve

- Melt the butter in a skillet with 1 tablespoon of the oil and sauté the shallots over medium heat for 3–4 minutes, until softened. Add the mushrooms and sauté for 3–4 minutes, until soft and golden.

- Sprinkle in the paprika and heat for 1 minute, then stir in the sour cream and peppercorns. Season to taste and simmer for 2–3 minutes, until slightly thickened.

- Meanwhile, heat the remaining oil in a large skillet and cook the steaks for 4–8 minutes, turning once, until done to your preference. Set aside to rest for 2–3 minutes, adding any juices to the stroganoff sauce.

- Arrange the steaks on serving plates and serve with the sauce, parsley, and cooked rice.

Stripped Beef and Mushroom Pan-Fry

Heat 2 tablespoons olive oil in a large skillet and cook 8 oz thinly sliced beef strips over high heat for 2–3 minutes, until browned. Transfer to a plate and set aside. Put 2 cups sliced mushrooms into the pan with 2 tablespoons butter and 1 chopped garlic clove and sauté for 2–3 minutes, until soft and golden. Sprinkle 2 teaspoons sweet paprika over the top and stir for 1 minute. Add ⅔ cup sour cream, simmer for 1 minute, and season to taste. Return the beef to the pan to reheat. Serve with the rice and parsley, as above.

Lazy Beef and Mushroom Stroganoff

Heat 2 tablespoons oil in a large skillet and cook 8 oz sliced sirloin steak over high heat for 3–4 minutes, until browned. Transfer to a plate and set aside. Put 2 tablespoons butter into the pan and sauté 1 finely chopped onion and 1 seeded and sliced green bell pepper for 5–6 minutes, until softened slightly. Add 2 cups halved baby button mushrooms with 1 chopped garlic clove and cook for 3–4 minutes, until soft and golden. Stir 2 teaspoons sweet paprika and 2 teaspoons all-purpose flour into the pan, cook for 1 minute, then add 3 tablespoons dry sherry and simmer until completely evaporated. Pour in ⅔ cup good-quality beef stock and simmer to reduce by half. Add ⅔ cup sour cream, a generous pinch of salt and black pepper, and 2 tablespoons chopped parsley. Bring to a boil, then return the beef to the pan and simmer for 2–3 minutes, until hot and tender. Serve with the rice and parsley, as above.

WIN-COMF-GYN

 # Cacciatore-Style Chicken and Salami Pasta

Serves 4

3 tablespoons olive oil
1 red onion, thinly sliced
2 garlic cloves, chopped
1 lb boneless, skinless chicken
  breast, thinly sliced
3 oz salami, thinly sliced and
  halved
½ cup red wine
2 rosemary sprigs, leaves chopped
2 (14½ oz) cans cherry tomatoes
 or diced tomatoes
¾ cup green olives (optional)
1 lb fusilli or other short pasta
salt and black pepper

- Heat the oil in a large skillet and sauté the onion and garlic over medium-high heat for 4–5 minutes, until slightly softened. Add the chicken and salami and cook for another 3–4 minutes, until lightly golden.

- Pour the wine into the pan and simmer until completely evaporated. Add the rosemary, tomatoes, and olives (if using) and simmer for 8–10 minutes, until thickened slightly. Season to taste.

- Meanwhile, cook the pasta in a large saucepan of lightly salted boiling water for about 11 minutes, or according to the package directions, until "al dente." Drain and pile into serving bowls. Top with the sauce and serve.

Cacciatore Chicken and Salami Ciabatta

Heat 2 tablespoons olive oil in a skillet and cook 1 lb boneless, skinless chicken breasts cut into thick strips over medium-high heat for 8 minutes, turning occasionally, or until cooked through and golden. Transfer to a plate and set aside. Meanwhile, cut 1 large ciabatta loaf into 8 sandwich slices. Divide 3 oz sliced salami among 4 slices of the bread. Slice 8 cherry tomatoes, ½ cup green olives, and half a small red onion. Put a little of each on top of the salami, then add some of the chicken and a small handful of arugula. Cover with the remaining bread and serve.

Oven-Baked Chicken and Salami Cacciatore

Prepare the cacciatore sauce following the main recipe, but omitting the chicken, salami, and olives. Bring to a boil and simmer for 4–5 minutes, until thickened slightly. Meanwhile, put 4 skinless, boneless chicken breasts between 2 pieces of plastic wrap and bash with a rolling pin to flatten slightly. Heat 2 tablespoons olive oil in a large skillet and cook the chicken over medium-high heat for 5–6 minutes, turning once, until golden. Transfer to a large ovenproof dish with the salami and olives from the main recipe. Pour the sauce over the top and bake in a preheated oven, at 425°F, for about 15 minutes, until the chicken is cooked through. Serve with cooked pasta, as in the main recipe.

 # Quick Fish Schnitzel with Tartar Sauce

Serves 2

½ cup dried bread crumbs
1 tablespoon dried parsley
½ teaspoon grated lemon zest
1 egg
2 tablespoons all-purpose flour
2 flounder fillets or other thin white fish fillets
3 tablespoons olive oil
salt and black pepper

To serve

tartar sauce
lemon wedges
cooked peas

- Mix the bread crumbs, parsley, and lemon zest in a shallow dish. Break the egg into a second dish and beat lightly. Place the flour in a third dish, add some seasoning, and mix well.

- Dip the fish fillets first in the seasoned flour, then the egg, followed by the bread crumbs, making sure each is well coated.

- Heat the oil in a large skillet and cook the fish over medium heat for 2–3 minutes on each side, until golden and flaky. Drain on paper towels and serve with tartar sauce, lemon wedges, and peas.

 ### Baskets of Fish Sticks with Lemon

Cut 2 chunky fish fillets into strips and coat with the flour, egg and bread crumbs, as above. Arrange on a baking sheet lined with parchment paper and place in a preheated oven, at 400°F, for about 15 minutes, or until golden and flaky. Pile the fish sticks into baskets with oven fries and serve with lemon wedges and tartar sauce, as above.

Staying-In Fish and Chips

Cut 4 russet potatoes into fries and put into a nonstick roasting pan. Add 2 tablespoons olive oil and a pinch of salt and black pepper and toss well. Roast in a preheated oven, at 425°F, for 20–25 minutes, until tender and golden. Meanwhile, coat 2 chunky white fish fillets in flour, egg, and bread crumbs, following the main recipe. Heat a nonstick skillet over medium heat and pan-fry the fish for 7–8 minutes, turning once, until golden and flaky. Drain on paper towels, then arrange on plates with the homemade fries and serve with tartar sauce and lemon wedges, as above.

30 Quick Creamy Ham and Ricotta Cannelloni

Serves 4

3 tablespoons olive oil
2 garlic cloves, chopped
2 (14½ oz) cans diced tomatoes
2 tablespoons tomato paste
pinch of sugar
2 tablespoons chopped basil
1 cup ricotta cheese
5 oz ham, diced
1½ (6 oz) jars sliced mushrooms,
   drained
½ teaspoon grated lemon zest
12 fresh lasagna noodles,
   halved widthwise
1 cup shredded cheddar cheese
salt and black pepper

- Heat the oil in a large skillet and sauté the garlic over medium heat for 1 minute, until softened. Add the tomatoes, tomato paste, sugar, basil, and a generous pinch of salt and black pepper and simmer for 5–7 minutes, until slightly thickened.

- Meanwhile, put the ricotta into a saucepan with the ham, mushrooms, and lemon zest and heat gently until warm but not hot. Divide the mixture among the halved lasagna noodles and roll up to form filled tubes.

- Pour half the tomato sauce into an ovenproof dish, arrange the cannelloni in it, then cover with the remaining sauce. Sprinkle with the shredded cheese and bake in a preheated oven, at 425°F, for about 20 minutes, until the top is bubbling and golden and the lasagna is tender.

---

10 Creamy Ham and Ricotta Pancakes

Put 1 cup ricotta into a saucepan with 1 cup cooked, pulled or diced ham, 1 cup cream of mushroom soup, and 1 tablespoon chopped basil and season. Stir over medium heat until hot. Spoon the mixture onto 8 prepared plain pancakes, then fold in half and arrange in a large ovenproof dish. Sprinkle 1 cup shredded cheddar cheese over the top, then put under a preheated medium-hot broiler for 2–3 minutes, until melted. Serve with crusty bread and a green salad.

20 Creamy Ham and Ricotta Penne

Cook 1 lb penne pasta in a large saucepan of salted boiling water for 11 minutes, or according to the package directions, until "al dente." Drain, reserving 2 tablespoons of the cooking water. Meanwhile, melt 4 tablespoons butter in a large skillet and sauté 3 chopped banana shallots and 2 chopped garlic cloves for 3–4 minutes, until softened. Add 3 cups sliced mushrooms and cook for another 3–4 minutes, until soft and golden. Stir in 1 cup cooked, chopped ham, 1 cup ricotta, ⅔ cup light cream, 1 teaspoon lemon juice, and 2 tablespoons chopped basil. Season to taste, bring to boiling point, then stir into the drained pasta with the reserved water. Spoon into warm bowls to serve.

WIN-COMF-REK

 Roast Beef Waffles

Serves 4

2 tablespoons olive oil
1 onion, chopped
2 carrots, finely diced
⅔ cup frozen peas
1 tablespoon tomato paste
8 oz rare roast beef, diced
1¼ cups good-quality beef stock
2 teaspoons Worcestershire sauce
1 teaspoon thyme leaves
   (optional)
8 toasted waffles, to serve

- Heat the olive oil in a large saucepan and sauté the onion over medium-high heat for 5–6 minutes, until softened.

- Meanwhile, cook the carrots in a saucepan of lightly salted boiling water for 5–6 minutes, until just tender, adding the peas for the final 2 minutes. Drain.

- Add the tomato paste to the onions and stir for 1 minute. Mix in the diced beef, beef stock, Worcestershire sauce, and thyme (if using). Stir in the carrots and peas, then simmer for 2 minutes, until thickened slightly. Spoon over the toasted waffles to serve.

Superfast Beef Casserole

Make the beef filling following the main recipe, adding 1 (15 oz) can rinsed and drained navy beans. Meanwhile, heat 4 cups store-bought mashed potatoes according to the package directions and stir in ¾ cup shredded cheddar cheese. Spoon the filling into 4 individual ovenproof dishes and top with the mashed potatoes. Put under a preheated medium-hot broiler for 6–7 minutes, until bubbling and golden.

Beef Casserole with Parsnips

Put 3 diced parsnips and 2 diced russet potatoes into a large saucepan of lightly salted boiling water and cook for 10–12 minutes, until tender. Drain and mash with ¾ cup shredded sharp cheddar cheese, 4 tablespoons butter, and 1 tablespoon chopped chives and season. Meanwhile, heat 3 tablespoons olive oil in a large skillet and sauté 1 chopped onion, 1 chopped carrot, 1 chopped leek, and 1½ cups diced cremini mushrooms over medium-high heat for 7–8 minutes, until beginning to soften. Increase the heat, add 1 lb ground beef, and cook for 2–3 minutes, until browned all over. Reduce the heat and add 1 tablespoon all-purpose flour and 2 tablespoons tomato paste, stirring for 1 minute. Pour in 1¼ cups beef stock with the Worcestershire sauce and thyme from the main recipe. Simmer for 4–5 minutes, until rich and thick. Transfer to a large ovenproof dish and top with the cheesy mashed potatoes. Sprinkle ¾ cup shredded cheddar cheese over the potatoes and put under a preheated medium-hot broiler for 6–8 minutes, until bubbling and golden.

30 Feta-Stuffed Chicken with Chile and Capers

Serves 4

1⅓ cups crumbled feta cheese

1 red chile, seeded and chopped

2 teaspoons rinsed capers

1 teaspoon grated lemon zest

¾ cup pitted olives, sliced

2 tablespoons chopped cilantro
or parsley

2 tablespoons olive oil

4 chicken breasts, skin on

4 lemon wedges

2 Romano peppers, halved
lengthwise and seeded

1½ cups couscous

salt and black pepper

- Put the feta into a small bowl and add the chile, capers, lemon zest, olives, cilantro or parsley, and half the olive oil. Season generously with salt and black pepper.

- Cut a pocket into the side of each chicken breast and fill with half the feta mixture. Place, skin side up, in an ovenproof dish with the lemon wedges and Romano peppers.

- Drizzle over the remaining olive oil and place in a preheated oven, at 425°F, for about 20 minutes, until the chicken is cooked and golden.

- Meanwhile, cook the couscous according to the package directions, fluff up with a fork, and fold in the remaining feta mixture. Spoon onto plates and serve with the stuffed chicken, roasted peppers, and lemon wedges.

10 Chile Chicken and Feta Rolls

Put 2 cups cooked, sliced chicken breasts in a large bowl with the feta, chile, capers, olives, and cilantro from the main recipe. Add 1 tablespoon olive oil, 2 teaspoons lemon juice, 3 cups arugula, and a pinch of salt and black pepper. Toss to combine, then pile onto 4 large, soft flour tortillas. Roll up the tortillas and toast them on a hot ridged grill pan for 4–5 minutes, turning occasionally, until warm and charred. Cut in half diagonally and serve with a tabbouleh salad or steamed couscous for a more substantial meal.

20 Pan-Fried Chicken with Feta and Capers

Put 4 skinless chicken breasts between 2 large sheets of plastic wrap and bash with a rolling pin to flatten. Put into a large, shallow dish with the chile, cilantro, and lemon zest from the main recipe. Drizzle with 1 tablespoon olive oil and a pinch of salt and black pepper and mix well to coat. Heat 2 tablespoons olive oil in a large skillet and cook the chicken breasts over medium-high heat for 7–8 minutes, turning once, until cooked and golden. Transfer to serving plates. Crumble 1⅓ cups feta cheese over the chicken and sprinkle with 2 teaspoons rinsed and drained capers. Drizzle with a little extra olive oil and a squeeze of lemon juice and serve with steamed couscous.

 # Spicy Sausage and Salsa Ciabattas

Serves 4

4 chorizo cooking sausages
  or similar spicy sausages,
  thickly sliced
4 ciabatta-style rolls, cut in half
salad greens, to serve (optional)

For the salsa

12 baby plum tomatoes, quartered
1 avocado, peeled, pitted, and diced
2 tablespoons chopped cilantro
2 scallions, finely sliced
2 teaspoons lemon juice
2 tablespoons olive oil
salt and black pepper

- Heat a large, dry skillet and cook the sausage pieces over medium-high heat for 7–8 minutes, turning occasionally, until cooked and lightly golden.

- Meanwhile, combine the salsa ingredients in a bowl and season to taste.

- Heat a ridged grill pan and toast the cut side of the ciabatta rolls in it until they are nicely charred.

- Sandwich some sausage and salsa in each roll, topping the filling with a small handful of salad greens, if desired.

---

2 Spicy Sausage and Onion Subs

Cook 8 spicy sausages according to the package directions, until browned and cooked through. Meanwhile, heat 2 tablespoons vegetable oil in a large skillet and sauté 2 thinly sliced onions over medium-low heat for about 15 minutes, until soft and golden, adding 1 finely chopped red chile (seeded if less heat required) for the final 4–5 minutes. Stir in 2 tablespoons chopped fresh cilantro and 2 seeded and diced tomatoes and season to taste. Spoon the hot onion salsa into 4 large, submarine-style bread rolls. Top with the cooked sausages and serve hot.

3 Pastry-Wrapped Spicy Sausages

Put 1 lb sausagemeat or sausages with their casings removed in a bowl, add 1 finely chopped chile (seeded if less heat required), 2 finely chopped scallions, and 2 tablespoons chopped fresh cilantro, then mix with your hands. Roll into 8 thin sausage shapes. Unroll 1 sheet of puff pastry and cut into 8 equal rectangles. Place 1 sausage on each piece of pastry, then roll up and cut in half to create 16 small sausage rolls. Put on a nonstick baking sheet, make 3 slashes in the top of each roll, and brush with beaten egg. Bake in a preheated oven, at 400°F, for 15–18 minutes, until the sausage is cooked and the pastry is puffed and golden. Meanwhile, combine the salsa ingredients as above and serve with the wrapped sausages.

Pesto and Meatball Tagliatelle

Serves 4

2 tablespoons olive oil

8 oz smoked bacon, chopped

8 pork sausages, casings removed

1 red onion, finely chopped

2 garlic cloves, crushed

½ cup red wine

2 cups tomato puree or
  tomato sauce

3 tablespoons red pesto

1½ lb fresh tagliatelle

salt and black pepper

freshly grated Parmesan cheese,
  to serve (optional)

• Heat the oil in a large skillet and cook the bacon over medium-high heat for 2–3 minutes, until lightly golden. Meanwhile, roll the sausagemeat into 24 balls. Add to the pan and cook for another 2–3 minutes, shaking occasionally, until lightly browned all over.

• Add the onion and garlic and sauté for 3–4 minutes, stirring occasionally, until beginning to soften. Pour in the wine and simmer rapidly for 1 minute, or until reduced by half. Stir the tomato puree or sauce and pesto into the pan with a pinch of salt and black pepper, then simmer for 7–8 minutes, until thickened slightly.

• Meanwhile, cook the tagliatelle in a saucepan of salted boiling water for 2–3 minutes, or according to the package directions, until "al dente." Drain and pile into 4 warm bowls. Spoon the pesto meatballs over the pasta and serve immediately with plenty of grated Parmesan, if desired.

---

10 Pesto Spaghetti Meatballs

Cook 1½ lb fresh spaghetti in a saucepan of boiling water for 2–3 minutes, or according to the package directions. Heat 2 tablespoons oil in a skillet and sauté 1 chopped onion and 2 chopped garlic cloves over medium heat for 5–6 minutes. Meanwhile, cut 12 oz cooked pork meatballs in half and add to the pan with 2 cups tomato pasta sauce and 2 tablespoons red pesto. Bring to a boil and simmer for 1–2 minutes, until the meatballs are hot. Serve with the spaghetti.

30 Baked Sausage and Pesto Ragu

Heat 2 tablespoons oil in a large skillet and sauté 1 finely chopped red onion and 2 chopped garlic cloves over medium heat for 3–4 minutes, until beginning to soften. Increase the heat slightly and add 6 sausages with their casings removed. Cook for another 3–4 minutes, breaking up the sausagemeat as it cooks, until browned. Pour in ½ cup red wine and simmer rapidly for 1 minute to reduce by half, then add the tomato puree or tomato sauce and red pesto from the main recipe. Simmer for 2–3 minutes until slightly thickened. Meanwhile, cook 12 oz dried tagliatelle in a large saucepan of salted boiling water for 7–8 minutes, or according to the package directions, until almost "al dente." Drain well and put into a large ovenproof dish. Pour the sausage ragu over the pasta, then top with 4 oz sliced mozzarella and a pinch of dried oregano. Drizzle with 2 teaspoons olive oil and bake in a preheated oven, at 425°F, for about 15 minutes, until bubbling and golden.

30 Greek-Style Lamb and Eggplant Casserole

Serves 4–6

12 oz penne or rigatoni
3 tablespoons olive oil
1 onion, finely chopped
2 garlic cloves, chopped
1 lb lean ground lamb
2 tablespoons tomato paste
½ teaspoon ground cinnamon
pinch of ground cloves
2 (14½ oz) cans diced tomatoes
¾ (10½ oz) drained chargrilled
   eggplants, coarsely sliced
2 tablespoons chopped parsley
1½ cup store-bought Alfredo
   sauce or cheese sauce
½ cup grated Parmesan cheese
salt and black pepper

- Cook the pasta in a large saucepan of boiling salted water for 10–12 minutes, until almost "al dente," then drain.

- Meanwhile, heat the oil in a large, deep skillet and sauté the onion and garlic over medium-high heat for 5–6 minutes, until softened. Add the lamb and cook for 2–3 minutes, stirring occasionally, until browned all over.

- Add the tomato paste and spices and stir for 1 minute. Add the tomatoes, eggplants, and parsley, then season and simmer for 10 minutes, until thickened.

- Transfer the lamb to a large ovenproof dish and top with the drained pasta. Drizzle with the Alfredo sauce or cheese sauce and sprinkle with the Parmesan before putting under a preheated medium-hot broiler for 7–8 minutes, until golden and bubbling.

10 Greek Eggplant Salad with Lamb

Rub 2 tablespoons oil over 8–12 lamb cutlets, then rub in a pinch of dried oregano and season. Put under a preheated medium-hot broiler for 5–7 minutes, turning once. Cut 5 tomatoes into wedges and put into a bowl. Add the eggplants from the main recipe, plus ¾ cup pitted olives, 1⅓ cups diced feta cheese, and half a small, sliced red onion. Stir, then sprinkle with ½ teaspoon dried oregano. Serve with the cutlets, drizzling them with olive oil and offering lemon wedges to squeeze over.

20 Quick Penne with Lamb and Eggplant

Heat 2 tablespoons olive oil and cook 1 lb ground lamb over medium-high heat for 6–7 minutes, stirring frequently until browned all over. Meanwhile, cook 1 lb quick-cooking penne according to the package directions, until "al dente." Add 1½ cups store-bought tomato and olive pasta sauce to the lamb with ¾ (10½ oz) sliced chargrilled eggplants and 1 cup crumbled feta cheese. Stir well to combine, then mix with the pasta. Divide among 4–6 shallow ovenproof dishes and pour 1½ cups store-bought Alfredo sauce or cheese sauce over the pasta. Top with ½ cup grated Parmesan and put under a preheated hot broiler for 3–4 minutes, until golden.

QuickCook
Winter Desserts, Sweet Treats, and Drinks

Recipes listed by cooking time

3

2

10

Apple and Ginger Crumb Cakes

Makes 10

½ cup dark brown sugar

1¼ sticks softened butter

3 eggs

1 piece preserved ginger in syrup, drained and finely chopped

1 teaspoon ground ginger

1¼ cups all-purpose flour

2 teaspoons baking powder

1 sweet, crisp apple, peeled, cored, and coarsely grated

For the crumb topping

¼ cup firmly packed light brown sugar

⅓ cup all-purpose flour

¼ cup rolled oats

1 teaspoon cinnamon

4 tablespoons butter

- Lightly grease a 12-section muffin pan or line it with paper liners.

- Put the sugar, butter, eggs, preserved ginger, ground ginger, flour, and baking powder in a bowl and beat together. Stir in the apple.

- In a separate bowl, mix together the sugar, flour, oats and cinnamon, then add the butter and rub together, using your fingertips, until the mixture resembles coarse bread crumbs.

- Spoon the batter into the prepared pan and sprinkle some crumb mixture over each muffin.

- Bake in a preheated oven, at 375°F, for 12–15 minutes, until risen and firm to the touch. Transfer to a wire rack and serve warm.

Apple and Ginger Smoothie

Pour 2 cups apple cider into a large blender, add 1 piece chopped preserved ginger, 2 tablespoons preserved ginger syrup, 2 coarsely sliced bananas, and 10 ice cubes. Blend until smooth and pour into a pitcher. Repeat to make enough to serve 6.

Apple and Ginger Muffins

Sift 2 cups all-purpose flour into a large bowl, with 1 teaspoon ground ginger, 1 teaspoon baking powder, 1 teaspoon baking soda, and a pinch of salt. Stir in ½ cup firmly packed dark brown sugar. In a separate bowl, beat 2 extra-large eggs with 1 piece finely chopped preserved ginger, 1 tablespoon preserved ginger syrup, 1 cup buttermilk, 4 tablespoons buttered, melted and cooled, and 1 peeled, cored, and grated sweet, crisp apple. Pour the wet ingredients over the dry ingredients and mix until barely combined. Spoon into a prepared muffin pan, as in the main recipe, and sprinkle with 2 tablespoons rolled oats. Bake in a preheated oven, at 350°F, for 18–20 minutes, until risen and golden and firm to the touch. Transfer to a wire rack and serve warm.

 Wintry Fruit Salad

Serves 4

2 blood oranges
1 sweet, crisp apple, cored
  and sliced
2½ cups pineapple chunks
½ cup sliced dried figs
⅔ cup pomegranate seeds
2 tablespoons spiced dark rum
  (optional)
1 tablespoon honey
½ cup walnut halves, lightly
  crushed or chopped (optional)

- Put the oranges onto a cutting board and slice off the peel and pith at both ends. Now cut away the rest of the peel and pith in the same way. Put the oranges onto a plate (to catch the juices) and carefully slice between the membranes to cut into segments.

- Put the orange segments into a large bowl and gently combine with the other fruits, reserving a small handful of the pomegranate seeds.

- Mix the rum, if using, with the honey and add the orange juice from the plate. Drizzle the juice mixture over the salad, mixing gently to coat. Sprinkle with the reserved pomegranate seeds and walnuts, if using, and serve.

Wintry Warm Fruit Compote

Heat 2 cups apple cider in a large saucepan over medium-high heat with 1 cinnamon stick and the spiced rum and honey from the main recipe. Add 3 cups mixed dried fruits, such as figs, prunes, apricots, and raisins. Bring to a boil, then simmer for about 12 minutes, until the fruits have plumped up. Let cool slightly, then spoon into bowls to serve. Alternatively, chill and serve cold with Greek yogurt.

Wintry Baked Fruits

Peel 2 blood oranges as in the main recipe, then slice thickly. Arrange in a large roasting pan with 6 halved and pitted plums, 2 quartered pears, and ⅓ cup dried figs. Combine 2 tablespoons spiced dark rum and 2 tablespoons honey with 1 small cinnamon stick and ⅔ cup apple cider. Pour the apple cider mixture over the fruits and bake in a preheated oven, at 400°F, for 20–25 minutes, until tender. Spoon into shallow bowls and serve warm with Greek yogurt or crème fraîche, if desired.

# Panettone and Butter Pudding with Raspberries

Serves 4

4 tablespoons softened butter
8 oz panettone (sold in Italian
  delicatessens), cut into
  ¾ inch slices
1 cup frozen raspberries
2 cups milk
3 eggs, beaten
¼ cup granulated sugar
1 teaspoon vanilla extract
sifted confectioners' sugar,
  for dusting
heavy cream, to serve (optional)

- Spread the butter over one side of each panettone slice and arrange, overlapping slightly, in a shallow, buttered ovenproof dish. Sprinkle the raspberries over the top.

- Pour the milk into a saucepan and heat until almost boiling. Meanwhile, whisk together the eggs, sugar, and vanilla extract in a large bowl.

- Pour the hot milk into the egg mixture, whisking constantly, then pour it over the panettone and bake in a preheated oven, at 350°F, for about 20 minutes, until just set and lightly golden. Dust with confectioners' sugar and serve with heavy cream, if desired.

Grilled Panettone with Raspberries

Spread 6 tablespoons softened butter over both sides of 8 thick slices of panettone. Heat a large ridged grill pan and toast 4 slices of panettone over medium heat for 2–3 minutes, turning once, until striped and golden. Remove and repeat with the remaining slices. Arrange on serving plates sprinkled with a handful of raspberries and serve immediately, drizzled with crème anglaise, if desired.

Panettone and Raspberry Winter Pudding

Grill the slices of panettone as in the 10-minute recipe. Arrange in serving dishes and dust generously with confectioners' sugar. Meanwhile, transfer 3 cups frozen raspberries into a large saucepan with 3 tablespoons granulated sugar and 2 tablespoons crème de cassis. Warm gently over medium-low heat, stirring occasionally until the raspberries begin to collapse and the sugar has dissolved. Remove from the heat and let cool slightly. Spoon over the grilled panettone and serve with heavy cream, if desired.

Luscious Prune and Coffee Cupcakes

Serves 10

2 tablespoons unsweetened
  cocoa powder
2 tablespoons boiling water
1½ teaspoons coffee extract
1¼ sticks butter, melted
  and cooled
2 extra-large eggs, beaten
½ cup firmly packed light
  brown sugar
⅔ cup pitted prunes,
  finely chopped
1 cup all-purpose flour
1 teaspoon baking powder
whipped cream, to serve
  (optional)

- Lightly grease a 12-section muffin pan or line it with paper liners.

- Put the cocoa powder into a large bowl, pour in a boiling water and coffee extract, and stir until smooth. Add the melted butter and stir well.

- Whisk the eggs and sugar into the cocoa mixture, then add the prunes and sift in the flour and baking powder. Gently fold together.

- Spoon the batter carefully into the prepared muffin pan and bake in a preheated oven, at 375°F, for 10–12 minutes, until risen and firm to the touch. Transfer to a wire rack and serve warm or cold with whipped cream, if desired.

Espresso Prune Puree with Greek Yogurt

Pour ¼ cup freshly made espresso-style coffee into a blender or food processor and add 1 (12 oz) package prunes, coarsely chopped. Blend until smooth and sweeten to taste with sugar or honey. Spoon the mixture over bowls of Greek yogurt and serve drizzled with extra honey, if desired.

Prune and Espresso Tiramisu

Cut 6 chocolate-covered mini cake rolls into thick slices. Arrange in the bottom of 6 attractive serving dishes, then drizzle 1 tablespoon cold, sweetened espresso-style coffee over each dish of cake. Chop 12 pitted prunes and divide among the dishes. Sprinkle 1 tablespoon coarsely grated semisweet chocolate into each one. In a separate bowl, beat together 1 cup mascarpone and 1 cup chilled, prepared thick custard or vanilla pudding mix with 2 tablespoons coffee cream liqueur (such as Kahlua). Spoon over the prunes and top each dish with another tablespoon grated chocolate and 1 sliced prune to decorate, if desired. Chill for 10 minutes before serving.

30 Orange and Lemon Curd Cheesecakes

Serves 4

1¼ cups crushed graham crackers

4 tablespoons butter, melted and cooled

½ cup orange curd

3 tablespoons lemon curd

1 cup mascarpone or cream cheese

¼ cup heavy cream

2 tablespoons confectioners' sugar, sifted

orange and lemon jelly slices or mixed fresh berries, to decorate

- Put the crushed graham crackers and butter into a bowl and mix until the texture seems damp. Spoon into 4 individual serving glasses and press down with the back of the spoon. Place 1 tablespoon orange curd on each cookie crust.

- Put the lemon curd into a bowl with the mascarpone, heavy cream, and confectioners' sugar and beat until smooth and thick. Spoon half the mixture into the glasses. Top with another tablespoon of orange curd followed by the remaining mascarpone. Chill for 15–20 minutes, then decorate with the jelly slices or mixed berries, as preferred.

1 Orange and Lemon Curd Creams

Arrange 8 broken ladyfingers in the bottom of 4 glass serving dishes and pour 1 tablespoon limoncello liqueur over each one. Let soak for 5 minutes, then top each one with 1 tablespoon orange curd. Meanwhile, beat 3 tablespoons lemon curd and 2 tablespoons confectioners' sugar, sifted, into 1¼ cups fromage blanc or ricotta cheese and spoon over the ladyfingers. Crush 12 amaretti cookies and sprinkle them over the orange and lemon curd creams to serve.

2 Orange and Lemon Curd Cookies

Put 1½ sticks softened butter into a bowl with ¾ cup superfine or granulated sugar, 1 extra-large egg, lightly beaten, and ¾ cup ground almonds (almond meal). Beat together, then add 2 cups all-purpose flour and mix to form a soft dough. Roll into about 24 balls, place them on 2 baking sheets lined with parchment paper, and flatten slightly. Make a dent in the center of each one and fill half the cookies with ½ teaspoon lemon curd and the remaining half with orange curd. Bake in a preheated oven, at 400°F, for about 12 minutes, or until lightly golden. Transfer to wire racks to cool.

WIN-HJPG-REF

Toasted Ginger Syrup Waffles

Serves 4

4 tablespoons butter
¼ cup heavy cream
2 tablespoons packed dark
  brown sugar
1 piece preserved ginger, drained
  and finely chopped
2 tablespoons preserved
  ginger syrup
8 Belgian-style or regular
  store-bought waffles
good-quality vanilla ice cream,
  to serve

- Put the butter into a small saucepan with the cream, sugar, preserved ginger, and syrup. Warm over low heat for 5–6 minutes, stirring occasionally, until the butter has melted and the sugar dissolved.

- Meanwhile, toast the waffles according to the package directions and arrange on serving plates. Top with a scoop of ice cream and serve warm, drizzled with the ginger syrup.

2 Ginger Syrup Pain Perdu

Prepare the ginger syrup as in the main recipe. Meanwhile, put 2 eggs into a large, shallow bowl with ½ cup granulated sugar and 1 cup milk and whisk until smooth. Dip 4 slices of slightly stale brioche or challah bread into the mixture, turning to coat both sides. Melt 6 tablespoons unsalted butter in a large, nonstick skillet and cook the bread over medium-low heat for 4–5 minutes, turning once, until golden. Arrange on plates and top with a scoop of vanilla ice cream, a dusting of confectioners' sugar, and a drizzle of the ginger syrup.

3 Ginger Syrup Sponge Cakes

Prepare the ginger syrup as in the main recipe. Grease four ⅔ cup ramekins or other individual ovenproof dishes and put 1 tablespoon syrup into each one. Put 6 tablespoons butter, softened, into a large bowl and beat in ⅓ cup granulated sugar, ⅔ cup all-purpose flour, ¾ teaspoon baking powder, 1 extra-large egg, and 1 teaspoon ground ginger. When creamy, spoon into the ramekins. Bake in a preheated oven, at 350°F, for 15–18 minutes, until risen, golden, and firm to the touch. Let cool for a minute or two, then carefully invert into serving dishes. Serve with a scoop of vanilla ice cream and the remaining syrup.

 Brown Sugar Plum Turnovers

Serves 6

1 sheet store-bought puff pastry

½ cup prepared custard
or vanilla pudding

1 tablespoon packed light
brown sugar

1 teaspoon ground cinnamon

2 tablespoons ground almonds

1 teaspoon finely grated orange
zest, plus extra to garnish

5 plums, halved, pitted, and
thinly sliced

1 medium egg, beaten

demerara sugar or other raw
sugar, to sprinkle

sweetened mascarpone, to serve
(optional)

- Line a baking sheet with parchment paper.

- Unroll the pastry and cut it into six 4 inch squares. Place on the prepared baking sheet and spread the custard or vanilla pudding over them, leaving a ½ inch border around the edges.

- Put the brown sugar into a bowl with the cinnamon, almonds, and orange zest and mix well. Add the plums and toss to coat, then arrange a diagonal row of them across the middle of each pastry.

- Brush the border with beaten egg, then bring 2 diagonally opposite corners together and press to seal. Brush the pastries with the remaining egg and sprinkle 1 teaspoon demerara sugar over each one. Bake in a preheated oven, at 400°F, for 15–20 minutes, until the pastry is crisp and golden. Serve warm with sweetened mascarpone garnished with grated orange zest, if desired.

Brown Sugar Broiled Plums

Halve and pit 8–12 plums, depending on their size, and arrange, cut side up, in a shallow ovenproof dish. Drizzle with 2 tablespoons orange juice, dust with 1 teaspoon ground cinnamon, and sprinkle generously with ¼ cup packed light brown sugar. Put under a preheated medium-hot broiler for 5–7 minutes, until the sugar is melting and golden. Let cool slightly and serve with sweetened mascarpone, if desired.

Brown Sugar Poached Plums

Pour 1¾ cups cranberry juice and 1 cup water into a saucepan with 1 small cinnamon stick, 2 strips orange peel, and 2 tablespoons packed light brown sugar. Stir over medium heat to dissolve the sugar, then add 8–12 halved plums, depending on their size, and simmer for about 10 minutes, or until tender. Let cool slightly and serve with sweetened mascarpone, if desired.

Melting Chocolate and Date Cakes

Serves 6

1 stick butter, plus extra to grease
²⁄₃ cup all-purpose flour,
  plus extra for dusting
5 oz semisweet chocolate,
  broken into pieces
½ cup chopped pitted dates
2 extra-large eggs, plus
  2 extra-large egg yolks
⅓ cup firmly packed light
  brown sugar
ice cream or whipped cream,
  to serve

- Grease six ²⁄₃ cup ramekins or other individual ovenproof dishes and dust lightly with flour, tapping to remove any excess.

- Warm the butter with the chocolate and dates in a small saucepan over low heat, stirring occasionally until just melted. Set aside to cool slightly.

- Meanwhile, put the eggs, egg yolks, and sugar into a bowl and beat with a handheld electric mixer for 2–3 minutes, until pale and thick. Sift the flour into the bowl and mix together, then fold in the chocolate mixture.

- Divide the batter among the prepared ramekins. Place on a baking sheet and bake in a preheated oven, at 375°F, for about 10 minutes, until risen and just firm (the top should still be slightly yielding). Set aside to rest for 1–2 minutes, then invert into shallow serving dishes. Serve with ice cream or whipped cream.

Saucy Chocolate and Date Brownies

Arrange 6 store-bought chocolate brownies in an ovenproof dish, overlapping them slightly. Stir ²⁄₃ cup pitted and chopped dates into 1½ cups warmed, Belgian-style chocolate sauce and drizzle the mixture over the brownies. Place in a preheated oven, at 400°F, for 7–8 minutes, until warmed through. Serve in shallow dishes with ice cream or whipped cream.

White Chocolate Chunk and Date Brownies

Melt 1½ sticks butter in a small saucepan with 8 oz semisweet chocolate, broken into pieces, stirring occasionally until just melted. Remove from the heat and stir in ²⁄₃ cup pitted, chopped dates. Beat 3 eggs in a large bowl with ¾ cup granulated sugar, until pale and creamy. Add the cooled chocolate mixture plus ²⁄₃ cup all-purpose flour, ¾ teaspoon baking powder, and 5 oz white chocolate chunks. Mix gently to combine. Line a 9 inch square brownie pan with parchment paper, letting it stand a little above the sides. Pour in the brownie batter and bake in a preheated oven, at 375°F, for about 20 minutes, until just firm to the touch. Cool in the pan, then cut into squares to serve.

Figgy Rice Pudding Brûlée

Serves 4

8 teaspoons good-quality
  fig conserve
2 cups chilled, prepared
  rice pudding
½ cup chopped dried figs
1 teaspoon finely grated
  lemon zest (optional)
¼ cup granulated sugar

- Set out 4 small heatproof dishes or ramekins and put 2 teaspoons of fig conserve into each one.

- Empty the rice pudding into a bowl and stir in the figs, along with the lemon zest, if using. Spoon into the dishes.

- Sprinkle an even layer of the granulated sugar over the puddings and caramelize it with a blowtorch or under a hot broiler for 1–2 minutes.

- Set aside for 1–2 minutes, until the brûlée hardens, then serve immediately.

Rice Pudding with Roasted Figs

Put 8 halved figs, cut side up, into an ovenproof dish. Put 2 tablespoons butter into a small saucepan with 2 tablespoons honey and 2 teaspoons lemon juice and heat gently until warm. Pour the sauce over the figs and bake in a preheated oven, at 350°F, for 15–20 minutes, until tender. Meanwhile, warm 2 cups prepared rice pudding in a saucepan over medium-low heat, stirring occasionally, until hot. Spoon into dishes and serve with the roasted figs.

Figgy Rice Pudding

Put ⅔ cup short-grain rice in a large saucepan with 3 cups milk, ¼ cup firmly packed light brown sugar, 2 tablespoons butter, and 1 teaspoon finely grated lemon zest (optional). Bring to a boil over medium heat, stirring frequently to prevent it from burning, then simmer for about 25 minutes, adding more milk if it seems a little dry. Add ½ cup chopped, dried figs for the final 5 minutes. Spoon into bowls and top each one with a spoonful of fig conserve.

Mulled Spice Apple Juice

Serves 6

6½ cups apple juice or apple cider
4 cloves
2 star anise
1 small cinnamon stick
1 inch piece of fresh ginger root, peeled and sliced
1 small orange, cut into thin slices
honey, to taste
¼–⅓ cup apple brandy (optional)

- Put all the ingredients, except the brandy, into a saucepan and bring to a boil. Simmer gently for 7–8 minutes, until aromatic, then remove from the heat.

- Add the desired amount of brandy, or omit completely for a nonalcoholic version. Serve in a punch bowl, if desired, and pour into heatproof glasses.

Spiced Apple Pie Cupcakes

Sift 1 cup all-purpose flour into a bowl, then sift in 2 teaspoons baking powder and 1½ teaspoons ground apple pie spice. Add 1 stick butter, softened, ⅔ cup firmly packed dark brown sugar, 2 tablespoons applesauce, 1 small peeled and grated apple, and 2 eggs and beat well. Line a 12-section muffin pan with paper liners and spoon in the cake batter. Bake in a preheated oven, at 375°F, for 12–14 minutes, until risen and firm. Meanwhile, put ⅔ cup heavy cream into a bowl and beat in ⅔ cup cream cheese, ½ teaspoon ground cinnamon, and 2 tablespoons confectioners' sugar, sifted. Serve the cupcakes topped with a dollop of the spiced cream cheese frosting.

Spiced Tarte aux Pommes

Unroll 1 sheet of store-bought puff pastry and place on a baking sheet lined with parchment paper. Brush with butter and bake in a preheated oven, at 375°F, for 8–10 minutes, until beginning to puff and turn golden. Meanwhile, peel, core, and slice 4 sweet, crisp apples and cut into thin wedges. Put into a large saucepan with 4 tablespoons butter, 2 tablespoons granulated sugar, and 1 teaspoon ground allspice. Cook gently over medium-low heat, turning occasionally, until tender and lightly golden. Spoon the apples evenly and attractively over the pastry, leaving a clear narrow border around the edge. Return to the oven for another 8–10 minutes, until the pastry is crisp and golden. Set aside to cool slightly, then brush the tart with 3 tablespoons melted apricot preserves. Serve with whipped cream and a dusting of ground cinnamon, if desired.

20 Chunky Double Choc-Chip Cookies

Serves 6–8

1¼ sticks butter, softened
1 cup granulated sugar
1 egg, lightly beaten
1⅔ cups all-purpose flour
¼ cup unsweetened
    cocoa powder
½ teaspoon baking soda
½ cup white chocolate chunks
½ cup semisweet chocolate
    chunks

- Line 2 large baking sheets with parchment paper.

- Put the butter and sugar into a bowl and beat together until pale and creamy. Beat in the egg, then stir in the flour, cocoa powder, baking soda, and chocolate chunks.

- Pile 8–9 spoonfuls of the batter onto each prepared baking sheet, spacing them well apart so they have room to spread. Bake in a preheated oven, at 350°F, for about 10 minutes, until slightly firm around the edges. Transfer to a wire rack to cool slightly before serving.

10 Chocolate Chip Cookie and Yogurt

Desserts Break up 8 oz store-bought chocolate chip cookies in a freezer bag by tapping with a rolling pin until crumbled but not powdery. Pour 1 tablespoon thick dark chocolate sauce into the bottom of 6 individual serving glasses. Put 1⅔ cups Greek yogurt into a bowl and gently stir through another ¼ cup chocolate sauce to create a marbled effect. Spoon half the mixture into the glasses, then top with half the cookie crumbs. Repeat with the remaining yogurt and cookie crumbs, then serve.

30 Chocolate Chip Cakes

Sift 1⅓ cups all-purpose flour, ¼ cup unsweetened cocoa powder, and 2¼ teaspoons baking powder into a large bowl. Add 1 stick butter, diced, and rub in with your fingertips until the mixture resembles bread crumbs. Finely chop 4 oz store-bought chocolate chip cookie dough and stir into the flour with ¼ cup white chocolate chips. Add 1 lightly beaten egg and 1–2 tablespoons milk, just enough to make a stiff but sticky and lumpy batter. Line 2 large baking sheets with parchment paper and spoon 10–12 mounds onto them, spacing them well apart. Bake in a preheated oven, at 400°F, for 18–20 minutes, until lightly golden. Transfer to wire racks to cool.

Freeform Pear and Blackberry Pie

Serves 4–6

1 tablespoon fine semolina or cornmeal

1 sheet store-bought, rolled dough pie crust

flour, for dusting

1 egg white, lightly whisked

3 ripe but firm pears, peeled, cored, and cut into wedges

1 cup frozen blackberries

2 tablespoons demerara sugar or other raw sugar

½ teaspoon ground cinnamon

½ teaspoon ground ginger

whipped cream or ice cream, to serve (optional)

- Line a baking sheet with parchment paper, then sprinkle the semolina or cornmeal evenly over the baking sheet. Place the pastry on a lightly floured work surface and roll into a circle about 13 inches wide. Transfer to the prepared baking sheet and brush with the egg white.

- Pile the pears and blackberries into the center of the pastry, leaving a 1½ inch empty border around the edge. Mix the sugar, cinnamon, and ginger in a bowl and sprinkle 1½ tablespoons of this mixture over the fruit.

- Lift up the plain border and fold it over at regular intervals around the fruit, making a tuck now and then to keep the pie a circular shape. The center of the filling will still be visible. Brush with egg white and sprinkle with the remaining sugar mixture. Bake in a preheated oven, at 425°F, for 20–25 minutes, until the pastry is crisp and golden. Serve warm with whipped cream or ice cream, if desired.

1 **Pear and Blackberry Layered Crunch** Put 2 cups crushed gingersnaps into a bowl with 6 tablespoons melted butter and mix well. Place 1 tablespoonful blackberry conserve or jam in the bottom of 4 individual glass dishes. Put 1 cup chilled prepared custard or vanilla pudding and ⅔ cup Greek yogurt into a bowl and beat together. Spoon half the mixture over the conserve, then sprinkle half the crushed cookies on top. Drain and slice 1 (14½ oz) can pear halves and arrange over the cookies. Layer the remaining custard and cookies as before, then serve, decorated with a few blackberries, if desired.

2 **Pear and Blackberry Fruit Gratin** Put the pears, blackberries, and spices from the main recipe into a large bowl, add 2 tablespoons packed light brown sugar, and mix well. Transfer to an ovenproof dish and put under a preheated medium-hot broiler for 4–5 minutes. Meanwhile, combine 1 cup prepared vanilla pudding with 1 cup Greek yogurt. Pour it over the broiled fruit and sprinkle with ¼ cup demerara sugar or other raw sugar. Put back under the broiler for 3–4 minutes, until the sugar is melting and beginning to caramelize.

Cinnamon-Spiked Raisin Scones

Serves 4–5

2⅔ cups all-purpose flour,
  plus extra for dusting
4 teaspoons baking powder
1 teaspoon ground cinnamon
pinch of salt
6 tablespoons butter, diced
¼ cup firmly packed dark
  brown sugar
½ cup golden raisins
¾ cup buttermilk
1 medium egg, lightly beaten
1 cup mascarpone mixed with
  ⅓ cup heavy cream (a clotted
  cream substitute), to serve

- Sift the flour, baking powder, cinnamon, and salt into a large bowl. Add the butter and rub in with your fingertips, until the mixture resembles fine bread crumbs. Stir in the sugar and raisins. Pour the buttermilk into the dry ingredients, mixing to form a soft but not sticky dough.

- Place on a lightly floured work surface and roll out to a thickness of about 1 inch. Using a 2 inch cutter, stamp out 10–12 circles.

- Arrange the scones on a large baking sheet, brush the tops with the beaten egg, and bake in a preheated oven, at 425°F, for 10–15 minutes, until risen and golden. Transfer to wire racks to cool, and serve warm or cold with the clotted cream substitute of mixed mascarpone and heavy cream.

10 Cinnamon and Raisin Drop Scones

Sift 1⅔ cups all-purpose flour into a large bowl followed by 1 tablespoon baking powder and 1 teaspoon cinnamon. Stir in 3 tablespoons packed dark brown sugar, then make a well in the center. Break 1 extra-large egg into a small bowl and whisk in 1 cup buttermilk. Pour into the well and whisk together until the mixture is smooth and thick. Stir in ⅓ cup golden raisins. Brush a large, nonstick skillet with a little melted butter and place over medium heat. Add tablespoons of the scone batter to the pan, give them a little space to expand, and cook for about 1 minute on each side, flipping them over once bubbles begin to appear on the surface. Cook for another 30 seconds, until golden, then stack up on warm serving plates and serve with a clotted cream substitute (see main recipe above) and dusted with a little extra cinnamon, if desired.

30 Cinnamon Raisin Sheet Cake

Put 1 stick butter, softened, into a bowl and add ½ cup granulated sugar, 1 cup all-purpose flour, sifted, 2 teaspoons baking powder, 1 teaspoon ground cinnamon, 2 extra-large eggs, and 2 tablespoons light corn syrup. Beat with an electric mixer until creamy, then fold in ½ cup golden raisins. Line a 9 inch square cake pan with parchment paper, letting it stand above the edges, and fill with the batter. Bake in a preheated oven, at 375°F, for 20 minutes, until risen and firm. Carefully lift onto a wire rack to cool slightly, then cut into squares to serve.

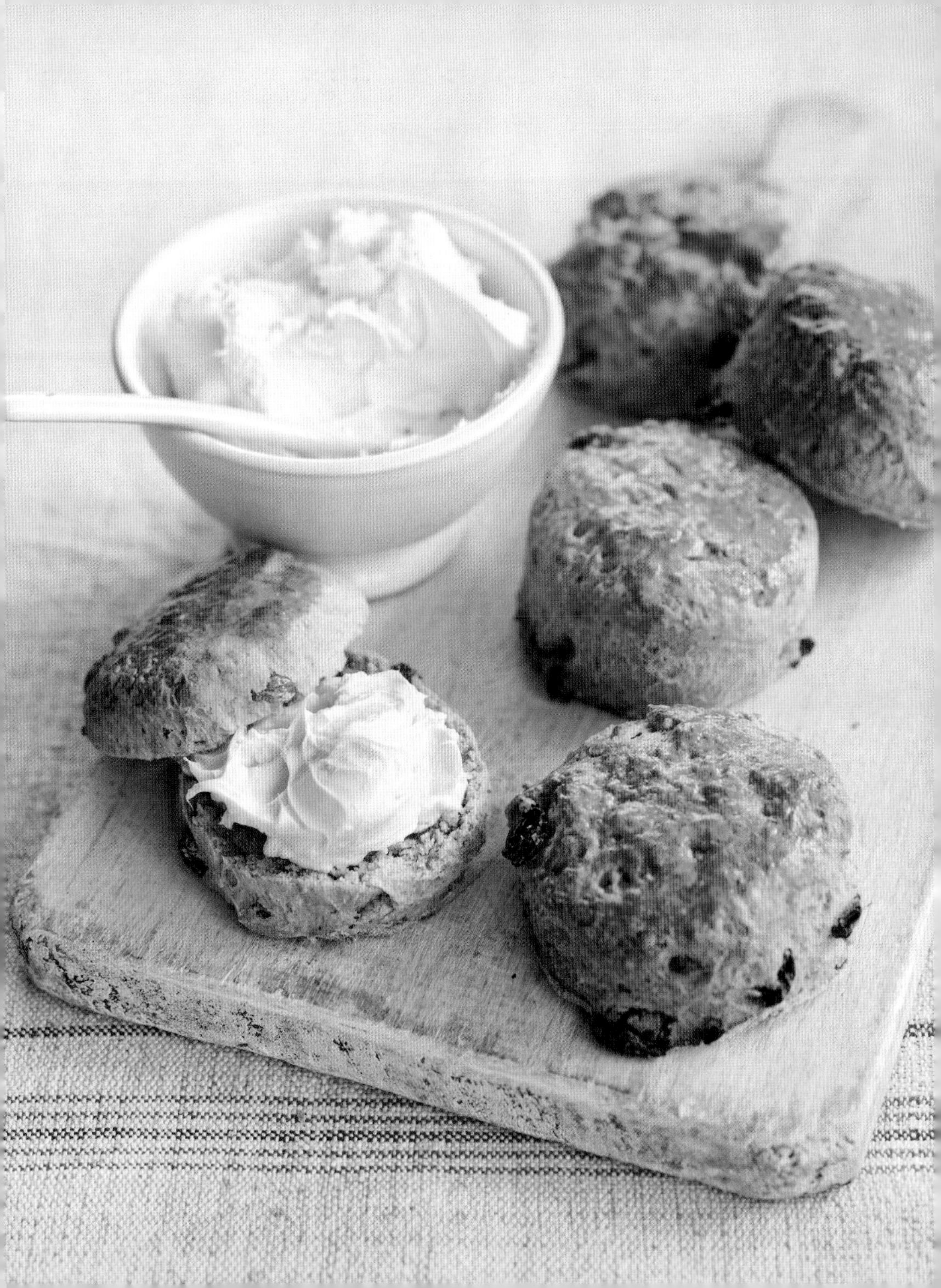

30 Mandarin and Vanilla Seed Brownies

Serves 6–8

1½ sticks butter

8 oz plain or orange-flavored semisweet chocolate, broken into pieces

3 extra-large eggs

seeds from 1 vanilla bean

⅓ cup firmly packed dark brown sugar

½ cup granulated sugar

⅔ cup all-purpose flour

¾ teaspoon baking powder

1 (11 oz) can mandarin oranges segments in juice, drained

- Line a 9 inch square cake pan with parchment paper, letting it stand a little above the edges.

- Warm the butter and chocolate in a small saucepan over low heat, stirring occasionally, until just melted. Set aside.

- Meanwhile, put the eggs, vanilla seeds, and sugars into a large bowl and beat until thick and pale. Sift in the flour and baking powder, mix well, then stir in the melted chocolate.

- Fill the prepared pan with the brownie mixture and sprinkle the mandarin segments over the top.

- Bake in a preheated oven, at 375°F, for about 20 minutes, or until just firm to the touch but with a slightly fudgy texture. Cool slightly in the pan, then lift onto a board and cut into squares to serve.

---

10 Mandarin and Vanilla Brûlée

Drain 2 (11 oz) cans mandarin orange segments and divide among 6 individual heatproof dishes. Put 1¼ cups crème fraîche or Greek yogurt in a bowl with 2 teaspoons vanilla extract, 3 tablespoons confectioners' sugar, sifted, and 1 tablespoon orange liqueur, such as Grand Marnier or Cointreau. Beat together, then spoon over the mandarins. Sprinkle 2 teaspoons granulated sugar on top of each dessert and caramelize with a blowtorch or under a hot broiler for 1–2 minutes. Serve as soon as the golden brûlée has hardened.

20 Homemade Vanilla Pudding with

Mandarins Put 4 extra-large egg yolks in a bowl with 1 teaspoon vanilla extract and ½ cup sugar and whisk together. Bring 1½ cups milk to a boil, then pour into the eggs in a steady stream, whisking constantly. Pour into a clean saucepan and place over low heat, whisking constantly until the pudding thickens; be careful it does not boil. Remove from the heat, stir ⅔ cup heavy cream into the pudding, and serve immediately with 2 (11 oz) cans drained mandarin orange segments.

1 Cinnamon-Spiced Banana Flambé

Serves 6

6 tablespoons butter
6 ripe but firm bananas, peeled
¼ cup firmly packed dark
  brown sugar
1 teaspoon ground cinnamon
⅓ cup dark or spiced rum
rum raisin ice cream, to serve
½ cup pecan halves, lightly
  crushed

- Melt the butter in a wide saucepan over medium heat. Slice the bananas in half lengthwise, add to the pan, and cook for 3–4 minutes, carefully turning once, until golden on both sides. Sprinkle with the sugar and cinnamon and heat gently to dissolve.

- Pour in the rum and carefully ignite it with a long match to flambé the bananas. Let the flames die out while spooning the liquid over the fruit.

- Arrange the bananas on warm serving plates with a scoop of ice cream, then sprinkle with the pecans and serve immediately.

2 Cinnamon-Spiced Banana-Caramel

Pecan Pie Put 1 cup pecan halves into a heavy skillet and toast over medium-low heat for 2–3 minutes, shaking the pan frequently. Add ¼ cup granulated sugar and 1 teaspoon ground cinnamon and stir occasionally, until the sugar melts. Simmer, without stirring, until the sugar turns golden brown. Pour the mixture onto a wax paper-lined baking sheet and set aside somewhere cool (not the refrigerator) to harden. Meanwhile, spread 1 cup thick salted caramel sauce or dulce de leche over a 10 inch sponge cake. Top with 4 sliced bananas. Whip 1 cup heavy cream with ½ teaspoon ground cinnamon and 2 tablespoons confectioners' sugar, sifted, until soft peaks form, then spoon over the bananas. Break up the caramelized pecans with a rolling pin and sprinkle them over the pie to serve.

3 Spiced Banana and Pecan Pie

Lightly grease a loose-bottom, 9 inch fluted tart pan and line with 1 sheet of store-bought, rolled dough pie crust, trimming off the excess. Put 2 extra-large eggs into a bowl, add 1 teaspoon ground cinnamon, ¼ cup granulated sugar, ⅔ cup light corn syrup, 2 tablespoons butter, melted, and 1 tablespoon lemon juice, and beat to combine. Cover the bottom of the pastry shell with 1 sliced banana and 1½ cups pecan halves. Pour the filling over the nuts and bake in a preheated oven, at 425°F, for 18–20 minutes. Cool slightly in the pan, then transfer to a plate, cut into slices, and serve warm with a scoop of ice cream, as above.

 # Rhubarb and Clementine Crisps

Serves 4

½ (32 oz) jar rhubarb pie filling,
    drained
1 cup (3½ oz) frozen raspberries
½ cup freshly squeezed
    clementine juice
1 piece of preserved ginger,
    drained and finely chopped
1 cup all-purpose flour
6 tablespoons butter
½ cup firmly packed light
    brown sugar
3 tablespoons rolled oats
2 tablespoons toasted slivered
    almonds
pinch of salt
raspberry ripple ice cream,
    to serve

- Combine the rhubarb and raspberries in a bowl with the clementine juice and ginger. Divide among 4 shallow, individual ovenproof dishes.

- Put the flour into a bowl and rub in the butter until the mixture resembles bread crumbs. Stir in the sugar, oats, almonds, and salt, then sprinkle this mixture over the rhubarb.

- Bake in a preheated oven, at 375°F, for about 18–20 minutes, until the topping is crisp and golden. Serve with a scoop of raspberry ripple ice cream.

10 **Rhubarb and Clementine Crunchy Whips** Crush 1 cup defrosted raspberries and spoon into 4 glass serving dishes. Put 2 cups Greek yogurt into a bowl with 2 cups drained rhubarb from a jar, 2 tablespoons clementine juice, 1 piece of finely chopped preserved ginger, and 1–2 tablespoons packed light brown sugar, depending on sweetness desired. Fold together, then spoon over the raspberries. Top each dish with a small handful of crunchy oat and nut cereal and serve immediately.

20 **Roasted Rhubarb with Clementines** Cut 10 rhubarb stems into 1½ inch lengths and put into a large ovenproof dish. Slice the peel and membrane away from 2 clementines, then cut into ½ inch slices and add to the rhubarb. Sprinkle with 3–4 tablespoons packed light brown sugar, depending on sweetness desired, then add the raspberries and preserved ginger from the main recipe. Roast in a preheated oven, at 400°F, for about 15 minutes, stirring once or twice, until tender. Remove from the oven and cool slightly

before serving with scoops of raspberry ripple ice cream.

Vanilla Cupcakes with Warm Blackberry Coulis

Serves 6

1 stick butter, softened,
  plus extra for greasing
1⅓ cups frozen or fresh
  blackberries
2 tablespoons freshly squeezed
  orange juice
¾ cup granulated sugar
2 teaspoons vanilla extract
⅔ cup all-purpose flour
¾ teaspoon baking powder
½ cup ground almonds
  (almond meal)
2 eggs
2 tablespoons heavy cream

- Grease a 12-section muffin pan.

- Put the blackberries in a saucepan with the orange juice, ¼ cup of the granulated sugar, and 1 teaspoon of the vanilla extract. Put over medium-low heat, stirring occasionally, until the sugar dissolves and the fruit collapses.

- Meanwhile, beat all the remaining ingredients together until creamy. Spoon the batter into the prepared pan and bake in a preheated oven, at 375°F, for 12–15 minutes, until risen and firm.

- Pour the warm blackberry mixture into a blender or food processor and blend until smooth. Pour into a pitcher.

- Serve the cupcakes warm with the warm blackberry coulis.

Blackberry and Vanilla Baskets

Whisk ⅔ cup heavy cream with 1 tablespoon confectioners' sugar, sifted, and 1 teaspoon vanilla extract until soft peaks form. Fold in ½ cup store-bought vanilla pudding. Put 1 cup blackberries into a blender or food processor with 2 tablespoons confectioners' sugar and 1 teaspoon vanilla extract and blend until smooth. Spoon the vanilla cream into 6 brandysnap baskets and serve immediately, drizzled with the coulis.

Blackberry and Vanilla Tart

Roll out 1 sheet store-bought rolled dough pie crust and use to line a lightly greased 9 inch fluted tart pan, trimming off the excess. Chill for a few minutes. Meanwhile, beat 1 stick butter, softened, with ¾ cup ground almonds (almond meal), ⅓ cup granulated sugar, 2 eggs, 1 teaspoon vanilla extract, ⅓ cup all-purpose flour, ¼ teaspoon baking powder, and 2 tablespoons heavy cream. Spoon evenly into the chilled pastry shell and sprinkle 1 cup blackberries over the top. Bake in a preheated oven, at 400°F, for about 22 minutes, until golden and firm to the touch. Serve drizzled with the blackberry coulis from the main recipe.

Caramelized Apple and Hazelnut Phyllos

Serves 4–6

1 stick unsalted butter

5 sweet, crisp apples, peeled, cored, and sliced into thin wedges

2 tablespoons packed dark brown sugar

1½ teaspoons lemon juice

3 sheets of phyllo pastry

2 tablespoons roasted chopped hazelnuts

caramel sauce, warmed, to drizzle (optional)

- Melt the butter in a large skillet and pour one-third of it into a small dish. Add the apples, sugar, and lemon juice to the pan and cook over medium heat for 7–8 minutes, turning occasionally, until tender and golden. Set aside.

- Meanwhile, brush each phyllo sheet with the reserved melted butter and lay the 3 sheets on top of one another. Cut the stacked sheets into 12 squares, then use these to line a 12-section muffine pan, arranging them at slightly different angles. Bake in a preheated oven, at 425°F, for 7–8 minutes, until crisp and golden.

- Arrange the phyllo pastry shells on serving plates and fill with the caramelized apples and roasted hazelnuts. Serve with warm caramel sauce, if desired.

---

2 American Apple and Hazelnut Pancakes

Pancakes Sift 1⅔ cups all-purpose flour, 1 teaspoon ground cinnamon (optional), and 2 teaspoons baking powder into a large bowl and make a well in the center. Break 2 eggs into a separate bowl, add ½ cup milk and 3 tablespoons granulated sugar, and beat together. Pour into the well and beat again, slowly incorporating the flour from the sides. Stir in 2 tablespoons chopped roasted hazelnuts and 1 small peeled, cored, and coarsely grated apple. Melt a small pat of butter in a large, nonstick skillet and pour in 4 or 5 small ladlefuls of the batter to form small thick pancakes. Cook over medium-low heat for 2–3 minutes, until bubbles start to appear on the surface. Flip over and cook for another 30–60 seconds, until golden. Repeat with the remaining batter to make about 18 pancakes. Serve warm, drizzled with maple syrup, if desired.

3 Apple and Hazelnut Strudels

Drain 1 (12 oz) package apple slices and put into a bowl with 1 teaspoon ground cinnamon, 2 tablespoons roasted chopped hazelnuts, 2 tablespoons packed dark brown sugar, and 1 teaspoon grated lemon zest. Mix. Butter and stack 3 phyllo pastry sheets as above. Cut each stack into 3 rectangles. Sprinkle each rectangle with 2 teaspoons ground hazelnuts, then spoon over the filling. Roll up, tucking in the edges. Bake the strudels on a lined baking sheet in a preheated oven, at 425°F, for 15–20 minutes, or until crisp and golden. Serve drizzled with warm caramel sauce.

Canned Cherry and Apricot Cobbler

Serves 6

2 (15 oz) cans pitted cherries
  in syrup
1 (15 oz) can apricot halves in
  juice, drained
2 tablespoons Amaretto liqueur
  or 2 tablespoons canned
  apricot juice
¾ cup all-purpose flour
1 teaspoon allspice (optional)
4 tablespoons butter, diced
2 tablespoons demerara sugar
  or other raw sugar
pinch of salt
1 egg, lightly beaten
¼ cup rolled oats
ice cream or whipped cream,
  to serve (optional)

- Empty 1 can of cherries into a saucepan with the apricots and Amaretto or juice. Drain the second can of cherries and add the fruit to the pan. Place over medium-low heat for 3–4 minutes, until warm.

- Sift the flour and allspice (if using) into a bowl and rub in the butter with your fingertips until the mixture resembles bread crumbs. Stir in the sugar and salt, then add the egg and mix briefly to form a dough.

- Pour the fruit mixture into a large ovenproof dish. Arrange small mounds of the dough over the top, then sprinkle with the oats. Bake in a preheated oven, at 400°F, for 18–20 minutes, until bubbling and golden.

- Spoon the cobbler into dishes and serve with ice cream or whipped cream, if desired.

---

10 Canned Cherries and Crunchy Oats

Put ¾ cup rolled oats into a bowl and mix with ¼ cup packed dark brown sugar, 4 tablespoons, melted butter, and ½ cup chopped nuts. Transfer to a large, nonstick skillet and toast gently over medium low-heat for 6–7 minutes, stirring frequently, until crisp and golden. Transfer to a plate and set aside. Meanwhile, warm the canned fruit with the Amaretto as in the main recipe. Spoon into dishes and serve topped with the crunchy oats.

20 Canned Cherry Crisp

Warm the canned fruit as in the main recipe. Meanwhile, combine the oats, sugar, melted butter, and chopped nuts from the 10-minute recipe, without toasting. Transfer the fruit to an ovenproof dish and cover with the crumb topping. Bake in a preheated oven, at 400°F, for about 15 minutes, or until the topping is crisp and golden. Serve with ice cream or whipped cream, as above.

10 Whipped Irish Cream Hot Chocolate

Serves 4

8 oz coarsely grated semisweet
  chocolate, plus extra
  for sprinkling
3¾ cups milk
⅔ cup heavy cream
1 tablespoon confectioners' sugar
⅓ cup Irish cream liqueur
1–2 tablespoons granulated sugar,
  according to taste

- Put the chocolate into a small heatproof bowl. Heat the milk in a saucepan until it is almost simmering.

- Meanwhile, whip the heavy cream with the confectioners' sugar until it forms soft peaks, then fold in 1 tablespoon of the cream liqueur.

- Pour about one-quarter of the hot milk into the heatproof bowl, stirring until the chocolate has melted. Add the remaining milk in a steady stream, stirring constantly. Add the remaining Irish cream and sweeten to taste with the granulated sugar.

- Pour the hot chocolate into mugs and top with the desired quantity of whipped cream. Sprinkle with a little extra grated chocolate to decorate, and serve immediately.

2 Spiced Irish Cream Latté

Heat 2½ cups milk in a saucepan with 1 small cinnamon stick, ¼ teaspoon ground nutmeg, and 2–3 blades of mace. Heat until almost boiling, then remove from the heat and stir in ⅓ cup Irish cream liqueur. Keep warm for about 10 minutes to let the flavors develop. Meanwhile, prepare 4 strong, espresso-style coffees in large mugs. Strain the spiced milk over the espressos and serve immediately, sweetened with sugar or honey, if desired.

3 Irish Cream Cup of Chai

Place 3 tablespoons loose black tea leaves in a large saucepan with 1 cinnamon stick, 4 cloves, 1 star anise, 3 crushed cardamom pods, 4 coriander seeds, and one ¾ inch piece of peeled and sliced fresh ginger root. Pour in 3 cups milk and put over low heat for about 20 minutes, stirring occasionally, without boiling. Remove the chai from the heat and stir in ⅓ cup Irish cream liqueur. Strain into warmed mugs and sweeten to taste with honey.

30 Fire and Ice Winter Berry Meringue Pie

Serves 6

2 cups frozen fruits

1 cup mascarpone

1 teaspoon vanilla extract

2 tablespoons confectioners' sugar

3 tablespoons crème de cassis or cranberry juice

1 (10 inch) sponge cake

3 extra-large egg whites

¾ cup superfine sugar or granulated sugar

raspberries or other berries, to decorate (optional)

- Line a baking sheet with parchment paper.

- Put the frozen fruits into a bowl or food processor with the mascarpone, vanilla extract, confectioners' sugar, and crème de cassis or cranberry juice. Beat or pulse until thick and smooth.

- Spread the fruit mixture over the cake in a thick, even layer. Place on the prepared baking sheet, then cover loosely with plastic wrap and chill in the freezer for about 15 minutes.

- Meanwhile, make the meringue mixture by beating the egg whites until they form soft peaks. Gradually add the sugar, a spoonful at a time, beating well between each addition, until the meringue is thick, glossy, and forms stiff peaks.

- Spoon the meringue mixture over the cake, using the back of the spoon to create peaks. Put under a preheated hot broiler for 1–2 minutes, until the top begins to brown.

- Cut into wedges, decorate with berries, if desired, and serve immediately.

---

10 Icy Winter Berry Meringues

Place 6 individual meringue nests on serving plates. Prepare the iced berry mascarpone as in the main recipe and spoon into the meringue nests. Top each one with a dollop of whipped cream and some berries. Serve immediately.

Icy Winter Berry Meringue Trifle

Cut 1 pound cake loaf into 1 inch cubes and arrange in the bottom of a large glass serving dish. Drizzle with ¼ cup crème de cassis or bluberry syrup and set aside to soak in. Meanwhile, prepare the iced berry mascarpone following the main recipe. In a separate bowl, whip 1 cup heavy cream with 1 teaspoon vanilla extract and 2 tablespoons sifted confectioners' sugar, until soft peaks form. Spoon the berry mixture over the soaked cake and cover with the whipped cream. Top with 16 mini meringues and a handful of berries, and serve immediately.

Sticky Citrus Friands

Serves 6

1½ sticks unsalted butter, melted, plus extra for greasing
5 extra-large egg whites
1 teaspoon finely grated lemon zest
1 teaspoon finely grated lime zest
2 tablespoons thin-cut orange marmalade
⅔ cup all-purpose flour
1⅔ cups confectioners' sugar
1¼ cups ground almonds
pinch of salt
2 tablespoons granulated sugar
⅓ cup freshly squeezed orange juice

- Brush one 12-section or two 6-section friand or cupcake pan(s) with melted butter.

- Beat the egg whites with the citrus zests and marmalade, until foamy but without peaks. Sift in the flour and confectioners' sugar, add the ground almonds, melted butter, and salt, and gently fold together.

- Spoon the batter into the prepared pan(s) and bake in a preheated oven, at 400°F, for about 12 minutes, until pale golden and firm to the touch.

- Meanwhile, put the granulated sugar and orange juice into a small saucepan over low heat and stir to dissolve. Simmer, stirring occasionally, until the juice becomes slightly syrupy, then set aside.

- Drizzle the syrup over the friands straight from the oven and let cool in the pan(s) until the syrup has been absorbed.

Sticky Citrus Muffins

Put ¼ cup marmalade into a small saucepan and add 1 tablespoon granulated sugar with 3 tablespoons freshly squeezed citrus juice (1 from a lemon, 1 from a lime, and 1 from an orange). Warm gently until the sugar has dissolved and the mixture is syrupy. Meanwhile, place 6 warmed lemon muffins in serving dishes. Drizzle the syrup over them and serve with a scoop of lemon or lime sorbet.

Sticky Citrus Cakes

Grease a 6-section nonstick giant muffin pan and put 1 tablespoon fine-cut marmalade in each cup. Put ½ cup granulated sugar into a large bowl with ¾ cup all-purpose flour, ¾ cup ground almonds (almond meal), 1 teaspoon baking powder, and ½ teaspoon baking soda. Put 1 stick cooled, melted butter into a separate bowl with ½ cup plain yogurt, 2 eggs, 1 teaspoon finely grated lemon, and 1 teaspoon lime zest. Beat well, then pour into the dry ingredients and mix gently until just combined. Spoon the batter over the marmalade and bake in a preheated oven, at 375°F, for 18–20 minutes, until risen and firm to the touch. Carefully invert the pan of cakes onto a large plate or board, then transfer each one to a serving plate. Serve with a scoop of citrus sorbet, if desired.

 # Moist Chocolate Pear Cake

Serves 6

6 tablespoons butter, melted and cooled, plus extra for greasing
2 (14½ oz) cans pear halves in juice, drained
½ cup milk
1 extra-large egg
1 cup all-purpose flour
1 teaspoon baking powder
3 tablespoons cocoa powder
⅔ cup granulated sugar
⅓ cup boiling water
rich vanilla ice cream, to serve (optional)

- Lightly grease a large ovenproof dish and arrange the pear halves in the bottom.

- Put the butter, milk, and egg in a large bowl and beat together. Sift in the flour, baking powder, and 2 tablespoons of the cocoa powder, add ⅓ cup of the granulated sugar and beat until smooth.

- Pour the batter over the pears and smooth with the back of a spatula.

- In a separate bowl, combine the remaining granulated sugar and cocoa powder with a boiling water and stir until smooth. Pour this mixture over the batter and bake in a preheated oven, at 400°F, for about 20 minutes, or until risen and firm to the touch. Set aside to rest for 1–2 minutes before serving with scoops of vanilla ice cream, if desired.

10 Chocolate Pears with a Crunchy

Topping Drain the pears from the main recipe, and coarsely dice the pears. Divide among 6 individual dishes and drizzle with 1½ cups of warmed, Belgian-style chocolate sauce. Top with 1 cup crushed, sweet oatmeal cookies and serve immediately with a scoop of vanilla ice-cream.

20 Poached Pears with Chocolate

Sauce Pour 5 cups apple juice into a large saucepan with 2 tablespoons honey, 1 teaspoon vanilla extract, and 2 teaspoons lemon juice. Put over medium-high heat until almost boiling, then add 6 peeled, cored, and quartered pears. Simmer for about 15 minutes, until tender. Spoon into bowls with the juice and serve drizzled with 1½ cups warmed, Belgian-style chocolate sauce and a scoop of vanilla ice cream.

 # Cinnamon Sugar Muffins

Serves 6

1⅔ cups all-purpose flour
2 teaspoons baking powder
1½ teaspoons ground cinnamon
1 cup wheat bran
½ cup granulated sugar
3 tablespoons demerara sugar
  or other raw sugar
2 extra-large eggs
1 ripe banana, mashed
4 tablespoons butter, melted
¾ cup buttermilk

- Line a 12-section muffin pan with paper liners.

- Sift the flour, baking powder, and ½ teaspoon of the cinnamon into a large bowl. Stir in the bran and granulated sugar. In a separate bowl, combine the remaining cinnamon with the demerara or raw sugar.

- Put the eggs, banana, butter, and buttermilk into a small bowl and beat well. Pour the wet ingredients over the dry ingredients and mix until barely combined.

- Spoon the batter into the prepared pan and sprinkle with the cinnamon sugar. Bake in a preheated oven, at 350°F, for 18–20 minutes, until risen and firm to the touch.

- Transfer the muffins to wire racks and serve warm.

---

1 **Cinnamon Syrup Pancakes**

Gently warm ⅓ cup maple syrup in a small saucepan with 1 teaspoon ground cinnamon and 1 teaspoon lemon juice. Toast 18 pancakes according to the package directions, then arrange on 6 plates in stacks of 3. Top each stack with a small sliced banana and a small handful of blueberries. Drizzle with the cinnamon syrup and serve with a scoop of vanilla ice cream, if desired.

2 **Cinnamon Sugar Cupcakes**

Put ⅔ cup granulated sugar into a large bowl, add 1 stick softened unsalted butter and 1 cup all-purpose flour, 2 teaspoons baking powder, 1 teaspoon ground cinnamon, and 2 extra-large eggs. Beat until pale and creamy. Line a 12-section muffin pan with paper liners and spoon the batter into them. Bake in a preheated oven, at 400°F, for 10–14 minutes, until risen and firm to the touch.

Meanwhile, combine 1 tablespoon confectioners' sugar with ½ teaspoon ground cinnamon. Transfer the baked cupcakes to a wire rack and sift the cinnamon sugar over them to serve.

Index

Page references in *italics*
indicate photographs

Acknowledgments

Recipes by **Jo McAuley**
Executive Editor **Eleanor Maxfield**
Senior Editor **Leanne Bryan**
Copy Editor **Trish Burgess**
Americanizer **Theresa Bebbington**
Art Direction **Tracy Killick for Tracy Killick Art Direction and Design**
Original design concept **www.gradedesign.com**
Designer **Tracy Killick for Tracy Killick Art Direction and Design**
Photographer **Will Heap**
Home Economist **Denise Smart**
Prop Stylist **Liz Hippisley**
Production Manager **Allison Gonsalves**